Through the Mutual Funds Maze

Through the Mutual Funds Maze

Introduction by Paul K. Bates,
Vice-President,
Personal Advisory Services,
Royal Trust

Grosvenor House Press Inc.
Toronto - Montreal

The Publisher wishes to express its gratitude to **Royal Trust** for an education grant which has made the publication of this book possible.

Canadian Cataloguing in Publication Data

Main entry under title:
Through the mutual funds maze
Includes index
ISBN 0-919959-37-7
1. Mutual funds — Canada.
HG5154.5.T57 1988 332.63'27'0971 C88-093847-1

Published by
Grosvenor House Press Inc.
111 Queen Street East
Suite 456
Toronto, Ontario
M5C 1S2

Éditions Grosvenor Inc.
1456 rue Sherbrooke ouest
Montréal, Québec
H3G 1K4

Cover design by David Sutherland
Cover illustration by Bryan Stewart
Printed and bound in Canada

Table of Contents

Publisher's Acknowledgements

The Publisher wishes to thank the authors for their ongoing cooperation. Grosvenor House Press also acknowledges the invaluable assistance of Ann Rhodes, Keith Douglas, and Paul Bates, Lauren Bradley, Mark Fitzgerald and John Crane of Royal Trust. Their advice and support were greatly appreciated throughout the process of preparing the manuscript for publication.

List of Contributors

Through the Mutual Funds Maze draws on the expertise of the following financial experts from across Canada:

PAUL K. BATES, Vice-President, Personal Advisory Services, Royal Trust.

DOUGLAS A. CANNON, partner of Fasken & Calvin, general income tax practice.

JOHN CRANE, Director of Investments, Royal Trust.

MARLENE DAVIDGE, partner of Toronto law firm Tory, Tory, DesLauriers & Binnington, member of the Policy Advisory Committee of the Ontario Securities Commission.

KEITH A. DOUGLAS, President, The Investment Funds Institute of Canada, author of numerous articles pertaining to investments and investment funds.

JOHN GRUNDY, Investment Manager, Commercial Union Assurance Company of Canada, contributing business writer for the *Globe & Mail, The Financial Post, Investor's Digest.*

NIGEL P. JOHNSTON, partner of Fasken & Calvin, general income tax practice.

ERIC KIRZNER, University of Waterloo Assistant Professor of Finance, contributing editor to *The MoneyLetter* and *The Hume MoneyLetter* (U.S.), widely published author of financial books, studies and technical reports.

MONICA TOWNSON, Ottawa-based economic consultant, author of *The Canadian Woman's Guide to Money*, contributor to *Moneywise*, *Canadian Living*, *The Financial Post*, *Your Money Magazine*, *Canadian Consumer*.

PEGGY WATERTON, budget planning and money management expert, owner of B.C.-based Dollars & Sense Budget Planners money management service.

INTRODUCTION

Why 1.5 Million Canadians Have Signed Up

by Paul K. Bates

"The reason the market is down today is because there are more sellers than buyers. The market is coming back. You watch. They've already discounted World War III in here." New York Stock Exchange trader George Abrams. Globe & Mail, Report On Business, October 20, 1987

"What seems to be clear is that in terms of risk and reward, it is still too soon to go back into the stock market." Globe & Mail, Report On Business, January 2, 1988

"Although we cannot rule out a slow-down in the North American economy, we still see no recession coming. Indeed we feel corporate profits for the next two quarters will be better than most analysts believe." Globe & Mail, Report On Business, January 2, 1988

"The decline in interest rates that is needed for good investment markets is likely to be elusive. Substantial improvements in the U.S. trade balance in 1988 will more likely reflect recession than economic growth." Financial Times of Canada, January 4, 1988

All of the above are excerpts from economic outlook statements made after the stock market crash of October 19, 1987. And if you find their language confusing, you're not alone. Financial writing is often confusing. (This book will *not* be confusing reading; that is our first guarantee.)

If you are thinking about investing in mutual funds for the first time or are currently investing in mutual funds and are uncertain where to go next, you are also probably not alone. Recent statistics show that more than one-fifth of all affluent Canadians own mutual funds. Yet many, particularly those who are at or near the peak of their "investing" years—mid-30s to late 50s—who are relatively well educated and have high household incomes, know very little about how mutual funds work, how these funds might fit their investment objectives and where to buy them.

And even those who once believed they were knowledgeable about mutual funds should forgive themselves if they feel a little confused today. The scene is changing; new funds and even new types of funds are coming into being all the time.

The growth has indeed been remarkable. Overall, mutual funds in Canada and the United States grew by an unbelievable 56 per cent in terms of funds under management between December 1985 and December 1987. During the same period, the number of funds from which to choose grew by 48 per cent.

Indeed, mutual funds have become one of the most dominant forms of investment for middle-income Canadians seeking a safe, diverse approach.

What is the reason for this increased popularity of mutual funds? There are several:

- Heavy advertising in recent years by many funds' distributors and management companies has brought about a significant increase in awareness of mutual funds.
- Stockbrokers have been much more aggressive in their efforts to sell mutual funds, particularly to smaller investors.
- Last but certainly not least, over the last five years many funds have turned in rates of return that have significantly outperformed the yields of savings accounts, term deposits and Canada Savings Bonds.

Throughout this period of growth, the considerable advantages that mutual funds offer investors have remained unchanged. There are six main ones.

1. The funds provide professional portfolio management at affordable prices. In fact, you will often find that the annual management, administration and brokerage fees are far less than the brokerage costs you would pay if you were investing independently.

2. They offer relative safety of capital through diversification. As a simple analogy, consider the difference between owning a 100-unit apartment building and a duplex. If your apartment building has one vacancy, you have a 1 per cent loss of income; if one side of your duplex is empty, you are down 50 per cent.

3. They are a means whereby those with only small amounts of capital available can invest in the stock market.

4. They provide more assured rates of return than most independent investors can achieve, because the large number of securities they hold reduces the volatility in return inherent in less diversified portfolios.

5. They provide automatic record-keeping (including the necessary tax return documents at year-end).

6. They are a long-term investment with short-term liquidity. Most funds have monthly or weekly redemptions, and many now offer daily redemptions.

As well, there is now a broad choice of funds to meet virtually every investment objective. The explosive growth in the industry has literally created a fund to answer every investor's need.

IT IS COINCIDENTAL, PERHAPS, that this book is written at this time, so shortly after October 19, 1987, a day that will be recorded in history as Black Monday, a day during which, in seven short hours, the markets around the world plummeted in a free fall never before witnessed. It is coincidental because, during the previous most catastrophic market collapse, in October 1929, many of the most severe losses occurred in closed-end investment trusts. These trusts were fast gaining popularity just as the stock market peaked. They were also the forerunners of the mutual fund.

What made the performance of closed-end trusts appear so devastating was the use of leverage, the practice of using borrowed capital to invest in order to benefit from rising stock prices.

The investigations that followed the crash of 1929 yielded some startling disclosures. For example, the portfolios of many of the closed-end trusts contained stocks which were of such poor quality that they would probably not have been saleable by themselves on the open market. (This had not been common knowledge because the trusts had not been required to issue regular reports on their portfolio holdings.)

All this created much uncertainty about market investments in general, and extreme lack of confidence in the closed-end trust in particular.

It was against this backdrop that the modern mutual fund was developed. In fact the ''open-end'' mutual fund has become the pre-eminent form of managed investment fund in Canada and the United States.

Closed-end funds still exist today (and are governed by far tighter regulations). However, two key differences between them and the open-end mutual funds remain:

- The unit or share price of a mutual fund has a constant relationship to the current net value of the assets held by the fund. The fund has an obligation to redeem units at this net asset value whenever they are tendered. By contrast, the price of shares of closed-end investment funds is established by the marketplace, just like that of regular stocks, which may not reflect the underlying asset value.
- An open-end mutual fund is continually issuing new units and redeeming existing ones. Closed-end funds issue a pre-set number of shares which are then traded on the market.

In addition, various regulatory bodies such as the Ontario Securities Commission have created extensive regulations which serve to inform and protect the prospective mutual funds investor.

In the United States, the first open-end mutual fund was launched in 1924 by the Massachusetts Investors Trust in Boston. In Canada, mutual funds began with the launch in 1932 of the Canadian Investment Fund by Alan Chippindale of Calvin Bullock, a U.S. investment management firm. However, Canadian funds did not begin to grow significantly in popularity until the 1950s.

In recent years, substantial new securities regulations have been introduced to ensure the appropriate and timely disclosure of material information, control of borrowing within the funds, accurate and timely reporting, regular redemption dates, standardized accounting principles, protection against conflict of interest and so on.

This new environment of disclosure, procedures and regular reporting helps to protect the investor and has led to a renewed confidence in mutual funds.

The growth in the popularity of mutual funds in Canada during the 1950s also made clear the need for a formal association to represent the industry and to play a role for the funds' managers and distributors similar to that provided by the Investment Dealers Association for the stockbroking and investment dealer community.

An organization, originally named the Canadian Mutual Funds Association, was founded in 1962. Today, the Investment Funds Institute of Canada (IFIC) represents more than 350 investment funds which in total manage more than $20 billion in assets on behalf of more than 1.5 million Canadians.

A non-profit organization, IFIC provides three major functions:

- It maintains active representation to federal and provincial governments, and to the various regulatory bodies on matters of policy, tax issues and securities legislation as it affects the mutual funds industry.
- It promotes and builds awareness of prudent investing in mutual funds.
- It maintains high industry standards of knowledge and information through development and administration of specialized education courses.

IFIC also provides many services to its members, including statistical assimilation and analysis and monitoring of political, legislative and regulatory developments. It also provides a forum for the development of industry lobbying efforts.

IN THE LAST FIVE YEARS alone, the value of mutual funds held by Canadians represented by IFIC has grown sevenfold to approximately $20 billion. The number of Canadians who own mutual funds has climbed from a few thousand to more than 1.5 million; and today there are more than 400 funds to choose from. As this book is published, more new funds will be entering the market, as reregulation in the industry encourages increased competition.

This is a prime reason behind Royal Trust's decision to sponsor the development and publishing of this book. As the number of funds proliferates, as they become yet more diverse in nature, and as they advance their respective claims with increasing energy, so decisions to invest in mutual funds become more complex.

In producing this book, the goal has been to draw together *all* the key information you need to make the right decisions about mutual funds—today, and as circumstances change.

We shall cover a large range of topics in this book: how mutual funds developed and how they work; how to determine and meet your financial objectives; the characteristics of different funds; the management of funds; the effect of taxation on your fund investments; how to read fund prospectuses and reports; different funds for different market conditions; evaluating funds' performance; choosing the fund that's right for you; and assessing the costs of buying mutual funds.

We believe this book will be especially useful for:

• Potential first-time investors who are interested in stock and fixed income markets but who have hesitated due to a lack of comprehensive information about mutual funds;

• Those contemplating using mutual funds in their regular or self-directed Registered Retirement Savings Plans (RRSPs);

• Active investors who are committed to regular re-evaluation of their portfolios as market conditions, and their personal circumstances, change;

• Investors seeking a way to invest in a particular market—precious metals or the Japanese market perhaps—but who want to reduce the risks inherent in more speculative single-market investments;

- Those who want to build an investment portfolio, but who can only put aside a relatively small amount of money each month;
- Investors who are approaching retirement.

In order to provide the fullest, most up-to-date information, we have worked with the publisher to pull together a group of contributing editors whom we believe to be among the most expert in Canada today on the subject of mutual funds.

In several places throughout this book, you will find that our experts have recommended types of portfolios, or asset mixes, to be held by investors at certain ages and life stages. They are not identical: no two people could be expected to have completely identical investment philosophies. But, given the blue-chip nature of our writers, you can be assured that they are all sound. In short, rather than dictating a single strategy that some readers may not feel comfortable with, we have presented several strategies, all valid, so that every reader can select the one with which he or she feels most comfortable.

By the time you have finished this book, it is our belief that you will be able to make an informed decision as to whether to invest in mutual funds and which fund or funds you should invest in to meet your financial goals. You will be able to assess the costs and relative performance of the funds that appeal to you, and you will understand which events and personal circumstances should trigger a change in your portfolio. You will, in short, have achieved mastery of an increasingly complex topic.

With no confusion along the way.

CHAPTER 1

How to Meet Your Investment Objectives

by Paul K. Bates

Why begin a book on mutual funds with a chapter on how to create and follow an overall financial plan? Because it is only from this foundation that one can establish clearly defined personal investment objectives which, when met, will deliver the cash flow and personal net worth that you will need to meet your lifestyle goals. It would be impossible to design a personal financial plan appropriate for everyone (and especially in one short chapter). This requires an in-depth analysis of personal and family circumstances. We can, however, offer an outline of the basic steps anyone should take before embarking upon a program of investing. Once these basic exercises have been done—and perhaps reviewed with a financial planner—you should have a clear picture of how you might use mutual funds to meet your financial objectives.

Net Worth Worksheet

CASHABLE ASSETS

Cash, Savings & Chequing Accounts	________
CSBs, GICs & Term Deposits	________
Cash Value Life Insurance	________
Other: ________	________
Other: ________	________
Total Cashable Assets	$________

MARKETABLE ASSETS

Common & Preferred Stock (Can.)	________
Common & Preferred Stock (Foreign)	________
Bonds (Corporate, Government, etc.)	________
Mutual Funds	________
Other: ________	________
Other: ________	________
Total Marketable Assets	$________

NON-MARKETABLE ASSETS

Business Interests	________
Other: ________	________
Other: ________	________
Total Non-marketable Assets	$________

TAX-SHELTERED ASSETS

RRSPs	________
RRIF	________
Other (i.e. QSSP): ________	________
Total Tax-sheltered Assets	$________

REAL ESTATE

Principal Residence	________
Vacation Property(ies)	________
Investment Real Estate	________
Total Real Estate	$________

OTHER ASSETS

Household Furniture & Effects	________
Automobiles & Boats	________
Jewellery & Furs	________
Collector Items	________
Other: ________________	________
Total Personal Assets	$________
	________
Total Assets	$________
	________
Total Assets (Forward)	$________

SHORT TERM LIABILITIES

Charge Accounts	________
Credit Cards	________
Demand Loans	________
Insurance Policy Loans	________
Taxes due this year	________
Other: ________________	________
Total Short Term Liabilities	$________

LONG TERM LIABILITIES

Mortgage(s) on Residence	________
Mortgage(s) on Vacation Property(ies)	________
Mortgage(s) on Investment Real Estate	________
Installment Loan(s)	________
Business Loan(s)	________
Other: ________	________
Other: ________	________
Total Long Term Liabilities	$________
	________
Net Worth (Assets Less Liabilities)	$________

ADDITIONAL ASSETS

Employee Pension Contributions	________
Total Net Worth	$________

ADDITIONAL ASSETS ON DEATH

Personal Life Insurance	________
Corporate Group Life Insurance	________
Canada Pension Plan Benefits	________
Employer Pension & Other Tax Shelters	________
Other: ________	________
Other: ________	________
Other: ________	________
Total Additional Assets	$________
Annuities	________
Other: ________	________
Total Additional Assets on Death	$________

A step-by-step approach to building a financial plan

Your financial portrait

The first step is to review your financial position right now and for the immediate future. Where do you stand today? Do you anticipate major changes? Ask yourself these questions, using worksheets as necessary to record information:

1. What is my current net worth (i.e., total assets less total liabilities)?
2. Do I have sufficient cash reserves—or liquid investments that can readily be turned into cash—if emergencies crop up? (Most financial planners suggest a reserve equal to three or four months' net income.)
3. Will my excess (or discretionary) cash flow be sufficient to meet my short-term objectives, e.g., a major appliance or furniture purchase or a vacation?
4. Over and above taking care of emergencies and short-term objectives, how much discretionary cash flow do I have left over for investing?

By the time you have worked through this exercise, you will have a fairly precise idea of just how many dollars you have available for new, or additional, investments. And if the answer is "precious few," you should ask yourself a further question: Are my existing investment assets working as hard as they possibly can?

Goals and objectives

The next step is to ask yourself what are your long-term goals and objectives. Among the questions you should ask yourself are the following:

1. What are my specific lifestyle goals, e.g., a major purchase such as a second home or a boat, frequent vacations in faraway places?
2. Would I like us to live in a better home, perhaps a larger one and/or one in a better neighborhood?
3. Do I need to plan for children's education expenses?
4. May there be a need to provide financial support to aging parents?

5. At what age do I want to retire?
6. What kind of lifestyle do I look forward to after retirement, and what income level will I need to support it?

Your answers here obviously will be less precise. But at least you have started thinking about the future and putting some rough dollar figures on it. (If you want to be a little more precise, rework those figures to take account of how inflation—you'll have to guesstimate an average annual rate—will increase your dollar requirements by the time they arrive.)

Tax planning

Take a moment to add up all your sources of taxation, especially federal and provincial income taxes. A careful review, perhaps done with professional guidance, may uncover ways to defer or substantially reduce your current and future tax liabilities.

It is important to be up-to-date on all the tax changes that occur; they are probably the single largest expense you face. They also have a major impact on investment planning since interest income, dividend income, capital gains and investment income from foreign sources are all taxed at different levels. You should also understand the role of taxation in investing in an RRSP or company pension plan, and the repercussions when funds are withdrawn.

Asset analysis

Are your assets positioned in the most effective way? Careful analysis may well show you opportunities to improve your discretionary income, perhaps by reorganizing your debts or using non-productive savings to pay down your mortgage more quickly. Establishing budgets and living within them may also increase your cash flow available for investment capital.

Also check to see whether your assets are protected against inflation. Merely to stay even, your investments must increase your personal net worth at a rate that equals the rate of inflation. Ideally, of course, you'll do better than that. Your analysis may well suggest you should look for a better rate of return elsewhere.

Insurance and estate planning

A sudden change in your health may reduce your income or even cause your early retirement because of long-term disability. Worse, your premature death could result in hardship for your family. Your plans should provide for protection against these events. This is also the time to review and, if necessary, update your will. Leaving inappropriate instructions or dying intestate (without a will) can have devastating effects on the value of your estate and hence on the income of your heirs.

These matters will be covered in more detail in later chapters in this book. Once you have completed these basic exercises, reviewing your situation in the short term and the goals you want to achieve over the long term, your next step is investment planning, in other words the construction of a well-balanced portfolio that provides liquidity, income and growth.

Investment planning

On Friday, October 30, 1987, Royal Trust ran an advertisement in *The Globe and Mail* headed "It's times like these that make us think . . . and think again." It was an unusual ad. It made no attempt to sell a single product or service.

The intent was simple: to put into perspective the events of the previous two weeks which had begun with Black Monday, October 19, and to use that perspective to emphasize the basic tenets of sound portfolio planning. Here, in part, is what the ad said:

> "Remember, the foundation of long term successful investing is the careful distribution of your wealth, using these cornerstones:
>
> • Your personal needs, such as income and cash requirements, future objectives, and tax planning considerations.
>
> • Risk, and how much, if any, you're willing to accept.
>
> • Your available assets and your anticipated income.
>
> • Your age, health, and family circumstances.
>
> Your goal may be a balanced portfolio which provides safety, income and growth, according to your needs. It should contain a variety of investments, which should, and will, change over the years according to your requirements; and as economic and interest rate conditions change. These investments may include bonds, stocks, term deposits, mutual funds, real estate, and other types of investments. Your decision on how to distribute these

investments will have a major impact on your total return over the years.''

The golden rule of the investment industry is the know-your-client rule. This rule stands for the commitment by investment professionals to learn as much as possible about each client's goals before making a single investment recommendation. How can you apply this rule to yourself? Here's one approach to determine what's important to you.

Growth

Is your objective to build on your existing assets through capital-gain/investments — to build up your capital for some long-term objective, such as a child's education, or simply a larger nest egg toward your retirement capital?

Income

Do you need regular monthly or quarterly payments in the form of interest or dividends to supplement your other sources of income?

Liquidity

Do your personal or family circumstances require that you be able to convert most or all of your investments into cash at very short notice?

Risk vs safety

Are you the type of person who is not comfortable with any situation which may cause your existing capital to decrease in value?

Diversification

Is it important that you never put all your eggs in one basket, instead spreading your capital over more than one type of investment?

Tax advantage

Because of your circumstances, is it important to seek out investments which can provide tax relief through more favorable treatment of income and capital gains?

Convenience

Do you plan to make all the investment decisions, would you rather have a professional money manager invest on your behalf or would you prefer a combination approach?

As you begin to answer these questions, it will become clear that there is no single investment strategy to suit everyone. For some, the best strategy is to pay off mortgages or other non-tax-deductible indebtedness as quickly as possible. For others, it is to satisfy retirement needs or preserve savings from the ravages of inflation. But there is a general order to implementing a personalized investment program, as the following steps summarize:

Do first

- Take out appropriate life, disability and property insurance
- Create an emergency fund, using savings accounts, readily cashable Canada Savings Bonds (CSBs) or short-term guaranteed investment certificates (GICs)
- Make maximum RRSP contributions

Do next

- Reduce non-tax deductible debt
- Make diversified investments in stocks, bonds, mortgages, etc.
- Buy secondary real estate, such as a cottage or a rental property, if the idea of investing in real property appeals to you.

Do last

- Make sophisticated tax-advantaged investments
- Make high-risk investments such as commodities, options, precious metals, etc.

Having answered the "know yourself" questions posed earlier, you should now review the following table to see how different forms of investment rank against the different objectives you may have:

Type of investment	Growth potential	Income potential	Safety	Liquidity	Ease of decision-making
High-risk	yes	usually low	poor	usually poor	difficult
Tax-advantaged (e.g., flow-through shares)	yes	variable	variable	usually poor	difficult
Real estate	yes	variable	variable	poor	difficult
Stocks	yes	low	variable	good	difficult
Bonds	variable	high	high	good	difficult
Insurance	poor	low	good	poor	easy

Clearly, not every type of investment will be of use to you in meeting your goals. The various types differ significantly in terms of growth, income potential, safety of principal, liquidity and convenience.

What impact should your age have on the mix of your portfolio? The following table provides a useful guide although, as we shall see shortly, other factors than age should be considered when selecting an investment mix.

Investment category	*Age*			
	20-30	*31-49*	*50-60*	*Over 60*
	Percentage			
Liquidity (CSBs, short-term GICs, T-Bills, Money Market Funds	15-25	5-15	5-10	15-25
Current Income (long-term GICs, bonds, mortgage funds)	35-55	25-35	45-60	50-70
Growth (stocks, growth mutual funds)	20-40	50-70	30-50	15-25

From time to time you may well be tempted to follow a hunch, or maybe a hot tip; however, your long-term investment objectives should always guide your overall strategy. If you wish, make a little room within your program for speculation, but understand the risks, and do not count on this risk capital as part of your overall plan. In my early days in the investment industry I worked as a commodities broker, and I can assure you that my clients who were speculating in these markets were doing it for fun, not as part of their long-range investment plans. In other words, they had taken a piece of their capital and chosen to use it as risk money.

Always remember, a 50 per cent loss requires a 100 per cent gain to get back to where you started.

Your risk comfort level

Some people, no matter what their age or income level, are never comfortable with risk. Others thrive on it. Your responses to the following statements will indicate which kinds of investments you will be comfortable with and which ones may worry you. If you agree with a statement, circle the number at the end of the statement. If a statement doesn't apply to you, simply ignore it and go on to the next.

1. I need all my income. I can't afford to use any of it to buy stocks or the like .... (3)
2. I know stocks are where my money will grow but I would need a professional to select them for me .... (1)
3. I'd like to get a better return, but I don't want to risk everything I've built up .... (2)
4. I have enough set aside for emergencies. I'd like to know how to make the rest grow a lot more .... (1)
5. I'd like to make some of my money earn more, but I like the security of term deposits .... (2)
6. I'd like to increase my income as much as possible ... (3)
7. I am nervous about price changes in the market ...... (3)
8. Day-to-day price changes don't bother me; I'm investing for the long term .... (1)
9. I'd like a balance between growth of my capital and reasonable income .... (2)

If you circled mostly 1s, your objective is growth, which means emphasizing equities, or equity funds, to generate capital growth over the medium to longer term.

If you circled mostly 2s, your objective is to achieve a balance between long-term capital appreciation and current income. This means a balanced portfolio of equity and bonds.

If you circled mostly 3s, you are primarily an income-oriented investor. You should emphasize safety of capital and fixed rates of return.

The role of mutual funds

So where do mutual funds fit in your investment planning?

Consider, first, the main reasons why many people are unsuccessful investing directly in the market. Primarily, they lack the experience, the training or the time to be truly proficient at it. And they don't have enough capital to diversify adequately.

This is where mutual funds can help. They provide continuous professional management and broad diversification, as well as excellent liquidity. Additionally, the management fees are often lower than the brokerage fees you would pay if you were to trade individual securities for your own account. As well, even a small investor can diversify further by having a portfolio of funds.

As already mentioned, the list of funds is very long. Each fund is characterized by a distinct set of investment objectives, fees and risk levels. Many of them are eligible for RRSP investment.

You'll learn more about the nature of various types of funds in later chapters. In the meantime, let's see how they might fit into some specific investment plans.

Sample portfolios

For our first example, let's assume you are young, say under age 30, married with two small children. You are in a good job with excellent prospects for advancement but you require most of your salary to meet your immediate income needs. You have just inherited $40,000 from your grandparents and want to invest these funds conservatively. Only later in life when your employment income is much higher will you be prepared to be more aggressive with your investments.

We would recommend the portfolio outlined below which along with the two that follow, has been structured in light of the market outlook at the time of writing (April 1988):

- 25 per cent equity or growth funds
- 25 per cent bond funds
- 30 per cent mortgage funds
- 20 per cent money market funds, CSBs or term deposits

This strategy puts the larger part of your assets into high-yielding but low-risk fixed-income funds (bonds and mortgages). Term deposits, CSBs or money market funds provide investment security and ready access to cash. While the overall portfolio should be biased to conservative investments, a modest amount should be invested in equities for growth. (Despite the market's tumble in late 1987, its historic long term trend is up.)

If this young investor has not already set up an RRSP, he or she should do so right away, beginning with term deposits insured by the Canada Deposit Insurance Corporation, which will provide a backbone for wealth and security.

For our second example, we will assume you are in your early 40s. Many of your immediate consumption needs have been met or can easily be satisfied out of your current income. You have built up a good pool of safe investments such as CSBs, term deposits and savings accounts. You can now afford to take more risk, with the objective of growth. We believe you should be working toward the following portfolio mix:

- 55 per cent equity or growth funds
- 20 per cent bond funds
- 10 per cent mortgage funds
- 15 per cent money market funds, CSBs or short-term GICs.

This portfolio offers plenty of growth potential, and your secure financial position will enable you to ride out the ups and downs in the equity market. The 15 per cent in cash-type investments gives you an immediate source of funds if needed and a reserve for future equity purchases during stock market declines.

As our final example, let's assume you are in your early 50s. You are in your peak earning years and can hence afford to take some risk. But you can see retirement on the horizon and therefore need to strike a balance. A good portfolio mix for you would be:

- 40 per cent equity or growth funds
- 30 per cent bond funds
- 20 per cent mortgage funds
- 10 per cent money market funds, CSBs or short-term GICs.

As you approach retirement, your goal should be to gradually reduce the equity portion of your portfolio and increase the fixed-income component, thus ensuring that the capital to fund your retirement income is increasingly secure.

CHAPTER 2

Mutual Funds: What Are They?

by Monica Townson

Successful investing takes time, money and expertise. You need to spend time selecting a portfolio of investments and monitoring them on an almost daily basis to make sure they are performing well. You need a fair amount of money so that you can buy a selection of stocks, bonds or other investments, spreading your risk and increasing the prospects of earning a good return. In fact, it is often said that the minimum amount you should have for a diversified portfolio is $100,000. You need expertise to select the investments and to know when to buy and sell those you select.

The alternative, as we have already seen, is to invest in mutual funds.

There are almost as many different types of mutual funds as there are types of investors: conservative, high-risk, speculative, balanced. But they all work on the same principle: Investors pool their money, which is then invested by a professional manager who makes the decisions about when and what to buy and sell.

If you'd prefer not to take too much risk with your money, you can choose a conservative fund whose portfolio consists of mortgages or bonds. If you want almost no risk at all, you'll choose a money market fund that invests only in government-backed Treasury bills (T-bills) or top-quality bank- and corporate-guaranteed deposits. If you're more adventurous, you might go for an equity-based fund, in which growth stocks form the basis of the portfolio. If you are attracted by gold or real estate, you can choose a specialty fund that invests only in gold or real estate. And if you like the way the Japanese economy seems to be humming along, you might invest in a fund where the entire portfolio consists of stocks of Japanese companies.

The choice is almost infinite. The risks and potential rewards will vary according to the type of fund you choose. And the return on your investment will depend on the skills of your fund manager.

An open-ended deal

An investment fund is simply an organization whose business is to invest other people's money for them. There are now more than 400 such funds in Canada. By far, the majority of these are the open-end mutual funds which are the main subject of this book. (There is also a small handful of closed-end funds, which we'll discuss later.)

''Open-end'' simply means you can invest directly in the fund (generally through a broker, financial institution or fund salesperson) at any time. You can also take your money out of the fund at any time. The money you pay into a mutual fund is added to the money contributed by other investors, increasing the fund's total assets. The number of shares or units you'll get for your dollars or the amount of money you'll get if you cash in your units will depend on the value of the fund's units at the time you buy or sell.

That value, referred to as the net asset value per share or NAV, is calculated by taking the current market value of all the fund's assets, deducting administrative costs, then dividing the resulting amount by the number of shares or units outstanding. Because many investors may be buying or selling units on a continuous basis, most mutual funds calculate their NAV on a weekly or even daily basis. (You can look up NAVs in financial newspapers which regularly publish mutual fund tables.)

The price you'll pay for a unit in a mutual fund will thus have a direct relationship to the market value of the investments held in the fund's portfolio.

Depending on the type of fund, your return as an investor may come from dividends or interest earned by the securities in which the fund has invested, and/or from an increase in the NAV by the time you sell or redeem your holding. Here's an example of how the system works:

Suppose you have $1,000 to invest and the value of the fund's units stands at $10 each. In this particular fund, there's a sales fee of 8 per cent (called a "front-end load") which comes off the top of your investment, leaving you with $920—enough to buy you 92 units. (If you choose a fund without sales fees—often called a "no-load" fund—the entire $1,000 will be invested, giving you 100 shares instead of 92.) Now, let's say that at the time you want to redeem, the fund's NAV has risen to $15 a unit. You'll get $1,380 back when you cash in your 92 units. (Some funds charge a redemption fee, sometimes referred to as a "back-end load." You'll learn more about fees of all kinds in Chapter 8.)

The more popular the fund, of course, the more money it will attract and the bigger will be its pool of assets. Some Canadian funds have assets of $1 million or less, while the biggest have assets of more than $1 billion. At the end of December 1987, for instance, Industrial Growth Fund had assets of more than $1.4 billion, Templeton Growth Fund's assets were valued at nearly $1.3 billion and Investors Mortgage Fund, Royal Trust Mortgage Fund and Investors Dividend Fund each had around $1 billion in assets.

For the investor, however, a far more important criterion than a fund's size is its performance record. These records are published regularly in the financial press. The average annual compound rates of return given show how an investment in the fund would have grown in value, *assuming all income earned had been reinvested*. The calculations do not take into account sales fees, which can be as high as 9 per cent of the initial investment in some cases, but they virtually always include management fees and expenses incurred by the funds.

The latest available mutual funds performance survey by *The Financial Post* appears as Appendix I on page 161.

Mutual funds and your RRSP

Many mutual funds are qualified investments for Registered Retirement Savings Plans (RRSPs) and Registered Retirement Income Funds (RRIFs). There is a criterion: RRSP-eligible funds may not invest more than 10 per cent of their assets in foreign securities.

RRSP contributions are tax-deductible (within certain limits), so you'll be able to claim a deduction for any money you invest in a mutual fund through your RRSP.

However, you'll pay tax later when you receive funds from your RRSP fund—whether you take all the money out at once, use it to buy an annuity providing regular monthly payments or to acquire a RRIF providing flexible income payments. In each case, you'll have to declare the income you receive and pay tax on all of it. This is why it is generally preferable to emphasize interest-bearing securities in an RRSP rather than those yielding capital gains or dividends.

Consider a capital gain first. If you make capital gains on a mutual-fund investment outside an RRSP, those gains will be subject to the new tax provisions which generally allow you up to $100,000 of lifetime capital gains tax-free. Beyond that limit, you'll pay tax on only two-thirds of any gain. (This taxable portion will increase to three-quarters in 1990.) However, all capital gains made in an RRSP will sooner or later be subject to tax.

In like manner, you'll get a tax break on dividends earned by an investment outside an RRSP, but all dividends received within your mutual-fund RRSP will ultimately be fully taxed.

However, since the new tax rules no longer allow us $1,000 of interest income tax free each year, interest earned either outside or inside an RRSP is ultimately treated in exactly the same way for tax purposes.

For these reasons, many advisers suggest that you should not hold in an RRSP investments on which you hope to make a capital gain (growth mutual funds, for example), or from which dividends eligible for a tax credit will be received. The conventional wisdom is that interest-bearing investments should be concentrated in your RRSP while investments made for capital gain or dividend income should be held outside the RRSP.

However, there is another school of thought. It takes the position that an RRSP is probably the only significant investment many people have. The rates of return on many equity-based mutual-fund RRSPs are much higher than on RRSPs based on savings deposits and guaranteed investment certificates. So in many circumstances, according to this school of thought, an equity-based mutual-fund RRSP may be one of the best ways of providing a good income for retirement, even with the disadvantages you may face on the tax treatment of dividends and capital gains.

A variety to choose from

The wide variety of mutual funds available subdivide into four basic types:

1. Growth funds. The objective of these funds is to make capital gains for the investor. The degree of risk and the potential for growth vary from one fund to another. Some invest in high-quality Canadian equities; others favor foreign stocks. The higher-risk specialty funds invest in gold, energy stocks, real estate or commodity futures.

2. Fixed-income funds. These funds pay a secure income since the underlying investments generally pay a fixed rate of return. They include preferred shares, bonds and mortgages. While there may be some capital gain to the investor, the objective is to achieve maximum income while preserving capital and minimizing risk.

3. Balanced funds. These, as the name implies, aim to have a balance of different types of investments; typically, they will hold common stocks for growth as well as fixed-income securities such as bonds. The objective is to maximize the growth of assets while also protecting capital from risk as far as possible.

4. Money market and savings funds. These funds invest in short-term money market instruments such as government Treas-

ury bills or bank guaranteed deposits. The aim is to provide current income for the investor without taking any risks with the capital.

Now let's look at each type of fund in more detail.

Growth funds

If you buy a growth fund, you're hoping to see a significant increase in the value of your investment. That might be achieved in a relatively short time if you're willing to take chances and invest in some of the higher-risk specialty funds. On the other hand, you might be willing to settle for slower but steady growth by investing in a fund that specializes in blue-chip Canadian securities.

Canadian equity funds

The largest group of mutual funds are those investing in the common shares of Canadian corporations. Many of the Canadian equity funds are eligible for RRSPs.

Some of the best Canadian equity funds have a good performance record over a long period of time. But it's important to remember that annual average rates of return over a 10-year period may be quite a bit different from the rates of return from one year to the next. That's why it's important to treat these funds as a long-term investment and not as a way of making a quick killing on the stock market.

Because of the October 1987 stock market crash, few equity-based funds did well when their asset value at the end of 1987 is compared with assets a year earlier. According to *The Financial Post*'s mutual funds performance survey to Dec. 31, 1987, Royfund Equity, sponsored by the Royal Bank of Canada, turned in a 1.8 per cent loss when December 1987 was compared with December 1986. But over a 10-year period to the end of December 1987, the fund yielded an annual average compound return of 18.1 per cent. Canadian Security Growth, one of the AGF group of funds, lost 3.1 per cent in the 12-month period, but showed an average annual compound rate of return of 18.4 per cent in the 10-year period to Dec. 31, 1987.

Growth funds vary in risk and growth potential according to

the selection of stocks that make up their portfolios. Some funds, such as Canadian Investment Fund Ltd., invest mainly in blue-chip, dividend-paying common shares and are therefore suitable for the more conservative investor. Others, such as Industrial Growth, are a bit more aggressive in their pursuit of capital appreciation. Some funds are widely diversified, investing in all sectors of the economy; others specialize in a particular sector, such as energy or natural resources.

U.S. equity funds

Some equity-based funds invest entirely in the common shares of U.S. corporations. If you think the United States economy will generally do better than ours, this kind of fund will clearly appeal to you. Like funds investing in Canadian equities, U.S. equity funds' investments range from blue-chip to high-growth and sector-specific such as high-tech or energy.

For instance, among the funds managed by AGF Management Ltd., AGF Special Fund invests only in U.S. equities as does AGF's American Growth. Over the 10-year period to the end of December 1987, these two funds earned an average annual compound rate of return of 21.8 per cent and 18.2 per cent respectively. Mackenzie Financial Corporation's Industrial American Fund earned an average annual compound return of 17.4 per cent in the same 10-year period.

International funds

Some funds invest in the securities of a number of different countries, the rationale being that while markets in one country may be doing poorly, those in another may be booming. By diversifying internationally, the fund manager hopes to find the best global buys. Investing in European, Asian and Australian shares, for instance, may offset any downturns in North American markets.

The managers of several of the international funds are based in London, where they are closer to the day-to-day movements of the European markets. The lives of all international fund managers are complicated by the fact that they must take into account both movements in stock markets and also movements in exchange rates that will affect the return to the fund's Canadian investors.

The international funds vary in performance. For instance, Bolton Tremblay International, with assets of $465 million, averaged an annual compound rate of return of 19.6 per cent over the past 10 years, although this fund dropped by 8.8 per cent in the year ending Dec. 31, 1987. Cundill Value Fund averaged 21.8 per cent a year in the same 10-year period and even gained 12.9 per cent on a one-year basis. One of the best known and certainly the biggest international fund is Templeton Growth Fund with assets of $1.3 billion and a 10-year average annual growth record of 18.0 per cent.

Specialty funds

These funds concentrate their holdings in one particular sector of the economy, be it in one specific geographic location or in one particular sector. Some specialize in precious metals or energy stocks, others in stocks of small companies or those of companies in one country such as Japan. Many of these funds are high-risk and very volatile. They have the potential for very big gains—and very big losses. The return on your investment may fluctuate widely from one year to the next—another reason for emphasizing that mutual funds should be regarded as long-term investments, not suitable for a "quick-in-and-out" strategy.

Among the specialty funds, the gold and other precious metals funds are probably the most volatile. Gold-based funds such as Goldfund and Goldtrust have portfolios which include gold bullion as well as shares of gold mining and gold exploration and development companies in Canada, South Africa and Australia. Goldtrust jumped 17.0 per cent in asset value per share in the year ending Dec. 31, 1987. Its 10-year annual average compound rate of return was 14.9 per cent.

Funds specializing in shares of Japanese companies have been popular because of the buoyancy of the Japanese economy, and many have performed well. *The Financial Post* reported in December 1987 that AGF Japan was the top-performing mutual fund over both the past 10 and the past five years, yielding average annual compound returns of 25 per cent and 33.6 per cent respectively.

Second place in the performance ratings was also held by a fund specializing in Japanese securities. Investors Japanese Growth returned an average 23.1 per cent over five years, 30.6 per cent over the past 10 years.

Both these funds did well in 1987, despite the stock market crash, reflecting investor confidence in the Japanese economy and the resultant strength of the yen. AGF Japan gained 27.1 per cent in the year to Dec. 31, 1987, while Investors Japanese Growth returned 26.8 per cent.

A number of international funds specialize in the securities of a region. Examples are Global Strategy Europe and Global Strategy Far East. Both these funds are managed by Worldwide Capital Management of Toronto.

Then there are funds such as Royal Trust Energy Fund and Canadian Gas and Energy Fund which concentrate on investments in the energy sector. Funds specializing in shares of companies in natural resources such as copper, nickel, other minerals and forest products include Canadian Natural Resources, Natural Resources Growth Fund and Morgan Resource Fund. Specialty funds such as AGF HiTech Fund invest in companies in the high-tech field, while others, among them Saxon Small Capital Fund, specialize in smaller companies with low capitalization.

Real estate funds

These funds invest in income-generating commercial and industrial real estate. About 10 such funds now operate in Canada, among them First City RealFund with a net asset value of $29 million, Toronto-based Counsel Trust Co. with assets of $67 million, Investors Real Property with assets of $132 million and Imperial Realty Growth Fund with assets of $10 million.

The investor's return comes from the income the properties earn plus capital gains realized when properties are sold, as well as interest on short-term deposits which the fund may also hold.

While equity funds can value their assets on a daily basis because the securities they hold are traded virtually every day, real estate funds have to base their NAV calculations on an assessment of the value of the real estate they hold. They do this by getting the properties appraised — sometimes quarterly, but more often annually. That makes these funds far less liquid than most other types of mutual funds. They often require advance notice if you want to redeem your units, and they may take several months to process your application. A real estate mutual fund is very definitely a long-term investment.

These funds also operate under different rules from other funds. For instance, a real estate fund may use borrowed capital (debt), as well as money invested by shareholders, to purchase real estate. Provincial securities commissions may set other special rules. For example, the Ontario Securities Commission regulates the way in which funds' property appraisals must be carried out and sets the minimum capital requirement at $10 million (versus the $100,000 required for an equity-based fund and the $350,000 for a mortgage fund).

Commodity funds

These are the most risky of the specialty funds. Investing in commodities involves buying futures contracts, usually with a down payment of about 10 per cent. If the price of the commodity goes up or down, the investor could double his or her money—or lose the entire amount.

In Canada, these are also the rarest of specialty funds. Several have operated in the past. Most had clauses stating that if assets fell below a certain level they were automatically liquidated and, when gold and silver markets dropped some years ago, they all went out of business. Currently, the Vancouver-based Mustard Seed Fund, a very small operation with assets of only about $1 million, is the only commodity fund being sold here.

Fixed-income funds

These funds invest in portfolios of bonds, mortgages and preferred shares that pay a secure income. As we'll see shortly, these investments may themselves increase (or decline) in value, providing the investor with a capital gain (or loss), but the primary objective is to secure maximum income while preserving the capital invested. To generate that income, fixed-income funds generally invest in high-quality bonds, mortgages or preferred shares. Often, these securities are government-backed, for example, residential mortgages issued under National Housing Act (NHA) guarantees or Government of Canada bonds.

Fixed-income funds are generally low-risk; they appeal to conservative investors and to those who want to use mutual funds as an RRSP or RRIF or as part of a self-directed RRSP or RRIF. The dividends or interest their investments generate together with any capital gain or increase in the value of the securities in the portfolio, provide the returns for the investor.

Bond funds

Many fixed-income funds concentrate on bonds. Some invest only in Government of Canada bonds, some invest mainly in bonds issued by major corporations, some include foreign currency bonds and some have a combination of all of these. Government bonds usually pay slightly lower rates of return than corporate bonds which are viewed as higher-risk.

What all these funds have in common is their conservative investment policy and their focus on maximizing income. Capital appreciation, while it may happen, is generally only incidental to the management strategy.

One exception to this approach is the specialty bond fund. One example of this genre is AGF Global Government Bond Fund. Its goals are to get high income for investors *and* secure capital appreciation by investing in bonds of countries whose currencies are expected to appreciate. Investing in bonds issued by the central governments of countries with developed capital markets, it achieved a 20-per cent increase in value in 1987.

The more conventional bond funds include AMD Fixed Income Fund with assets of $52 million, Canadian Trusteed Income Fund with assets of $327 million, Investors Bond Fund with assets of $521 million, Dynamic Income Fund with assets of $79 million, Royal Trust Bond Fund with assets of $285 million and Royfund Bond Fund, sponsored by the Royal Bank of Canada, with assets of $236 million.

Not surprisingly, the performance of these funds does not match the spectacular heights of some of the equity-based funds. But they all weathered the 1987 market crash well and their performance over longer periods has been noteworthy. For instance, Investors Bond Fund increased in value by 2.7 per cent in the year to Dec. 31, 1987, and showed an annual return averaging 11.4 per cent for the five-year period to that date. Comparable gains at Dynamic Income Fund were 5.5 per cent and 12.1 per cent. Royfund Bond Fund gained 4.4 per cent over the year, and 10.3 per cent for the previous 10-year period.

Interest rates do much to determine the value of fixed-income investments. When interest rates go up, the value of fixed-income securities goes down and vice versa. Here's how it works.

Suppose you buy an Ontario Hydro bond maturing in August 1989. The stated interest rate on this bond is 13.75 per cent. When these bonds were issued some years earlier, this rate was in line with others prevailing in thc market, and the bond would have been attractive to investors. But since then, interest rates have fallen. A bond paying 13.75 per cent a year would, by late 1987, have been even more attractive because that rate was much higher than those currently available. For this reason, you will have to pay a premium for the bond. Instead of buying it at \$1,000—its face value—you may have to pay \$1,060 (again, at late 1987 market prices). The return on your investment will be 13.75 per cent of the face value, or \$137.50 a year. But when you factor in the premium you had to pay for the bond, the return will be much less than 13.75 per cent. On this particular bond, if you held it until maturity, the yield would work out to about 10 per cent a year—more in line with currently prevailing interest rates.

The successful manager of a bond fund will try to take advantage of interest rate trends to improve the yield of the portfolio. The manager's ability to call these trends correctly will have a large bearing on the performance of the fund.

Mortgage funds

These funds hold a portfolio of mortgages, typically first mortgages on residential property.

Broadly speaking, there are two types of residential mortgages. A "conventional" mortgage is a loan which typically does not exceed 75 per cent of the appraised value of the home. An "insured" mortgage is a loan that exceeds 75 per cent of appraised value requiring the mortgage to be insured against default by the borrower. The Canada Mortgage and Housing

Corporation (CMHC) is an organization which administers the National Housing Act and provides the insurance on payment or an insurance premium by the borrower.

Mortgage funds may hold both types of mortgage in their portfolios. Some, such as First Canadian Mortgage Fund sponsored by the Bank of Montreal, limit themselves to NHA mortgages and conventional mortgages that do not exceed 75 per cent of the property's value. Mortgage funds sponsored by financial institutions, such as Royal Trust's Mortgage Fund, will hold a selection of mortgages issued by that institution. While almost all funds confine their investments to residential mortgages, a few, among them London Life Mortgage Fund, also hold commercial and industrial mortgages.

The interest rate on mortgages is fixed when the loan is first issued. But in these days of rapidly changing interest rates, few residential mortgages are issued for terms of longer than five years and some have only a six-month term. The fund manager may have a mix of term lengths in the portfolio and will try to vary the mix to take advantage of interest-rate trends. But, while bonds are traded daily on the market, there is no such ready market for mortgages. So the manager of a mortgage fund is not able to take quite as much advantage of rate trends as might a bond fund's manager.

Like bond funds, mortgage funds weathered the crash well. Their longer-term rates of return, however, are more modest than those of equity-based funds. Here are the average annual compound returns, made over a one-year and a 10-year period respectively, reported as of December 31, 1987 by some of the major mortgage funds: Central Trust, 6.3 per cent and 10.6 per cent; First Canadian, 8.9 per cent and 14.3 per cent; Investors, 7.4 per cent and 11.1 per cent; Royal Trust, 8.0 per cent and 11.4 per cent.

Mortgage/bond funds

A number of funds combine bonds and mortgages in their portfolios. Some fix the percentage that will be in each type of investment; others vary the mix to suit market circumstances. Some funds also have dividend-paying common and preferred shares in their asset mix to maximize income and provide for some capital appreciation too. One example is Mackenzie Mortgage and Income Fund, which showed a return of 1.6 per cent in the year to Dec. 31, 1987, and earned an average annual compound rate of return of 11.6 per cent in the 10-year period to that date. Among other combined bond funds are Bolton Tremblay Bond and Mortgage Fund and Canada Life Fixed Income S-19 Fund.

Preferred dividend funds

These funds invest in high-quality preferred shares and sometimes dividend-paying common sharcs of taxable Canadian corporations. Their objective is to maximize dividend income for investors. The favourable tax treatment of dividends as opposed to interest, is appealing to many fund investors—although, as we saw earlier, usually not to those buying a mutual fund to hold as an RRSP or as part of a self-directed RRSP.

If you're looking at degrees of risk, preferred shares generally carry more risk than a corporation's bonds or debentures but they are generally more secure than common shares. A preferred share carries a fixed dividend, whereas a common share does not. Preferred shareholders also rank before common shareholders (but after bondholders) in their claims on the company in the event of liquidation.

That said, there is rather a confusing array of preferred shares, varying in risk and potential returns. Here are some of the varieties:

- Cumulative and non-cumulative. If a preferred share is "cumulative", it means that any time the company does not have enough money to pay the promised dividend, the shareholder's right to it carries over. When the company's financial situation improves, the missed dividends must be paid before any dividends are paid to holders of common shares. "Non-cumulative" simply means that if the dividend is missed it's gone forever.
- Retractable preferreds give the investor the option of tendering the shares for redemption at a specified price on a specified date. In effect, they have a maturity date, just as bonds do.
- Floating-rate preferred shares. Here, the dividend is fixed not as a percentage of the share's face value but in relation to

another measure, such as a percentage of the prime interest rate set each week by the Bank of Canada. In some cases, the dividend may not fall below a fixed minimum for a certain period of time.

• Sinking-fund preferreds. A company issuing this type of share sets up a fund which it will use to buy back the shares over a specified period. It may buy the shares on the market at a price not exceeding the stated redemption price. If it cannot buy back all the shares within the specified time, it may eventually call in the shares for redemption at the specified price. A sinking fund usually improves the marketability of preferred shares because investors know *someone* will be interested in buying their shares. This may also improve the shares price.

• Convertible preferreds. Buyers of these shares are guaranteed the right to convert them to some other type of security — usually a common share — over a specific period. Investors who are attracted to these shares because of the fixed dividend may subsequently decide to convert them to common shares if the company starts paying a higher dividend on its common shares, or if those shares have appreciated in value.

A preferred dividend fund may have a mix of all these types of preferreds in its portfolio. The objective remains to maximize dividend income.

While the preferred dividend funds did not perform as well as other fixed-income funds during 1987, some managed to make modest gains. For instance, Investors Dividend Fund gained 0.9 per cent in the year to Dec. 31, posting an average annual compound rate of return of 11.8 per cent for the 10-year period to the end of 1987. At PH & N Dividend Income Fund, offered by Vancouver-based Phillips, Hager and North, comparable gains were 6.2 per cent and 11.7 per cent.

Balanced funds

Balanced funds aim to achieve both income and capital appreciation while also preserving the capital invested. Their portfolios contain a mix of investments. Common shares will be included to provide diversification and growth potential. Some may also provide dividend income. Preferred shares may be included to increase income. Bonds and other fixed-income securities will be included for stability and income.

The fund manager will vary the balance between higher-risk growth securities and lower-risk fixed-income holdings to respond to changing market conditions. A balanced fund will usually be less volatile than a fund holding only common shares. It will appeal to investors who would like to have a mix of assets in their portfolio.

Some balanced funds were caught off balance by the 1987 crash, but still look fairly good over the long haul. For instance, the CMA RSP Balanced Fund earned an average annual compound return of 13.1 per cent in the five-year period ending Dec. 31, 1987, but it returned only 3.1 per cent during 1987, reflecting the impact of the October 1987 stock market crash.

Money market and savings funds

Mutual funds based on money markets and savings deposits are the lowest-risk of all. Their objective is to provide current income without taking any risks with capital. In periods when stock markets are fluctuating wildly, money market funds are particularly appealing. Not surprisingly in the light of current maket conditions, these funds are among the fastest-growing in both Canada and the United States. For example, Royal Trust's Money Market Fund attracted more than $100 million in the first six months of its existence.

These funds build their portfolios from quite a wide variety of investments. In the money markets, they may invest in Government of Canada or provincial government Treasury bills, issued for terms of up to one year. These investments are sold at a discount; the return to the investor is the difference between the purchase price and the full face value which is paid when the bill matures. The Bank of Canada prime rate is set each Thursday according to the current yield on Government of Canada T-bills, so these investments can be counted on to yield a return that moves in close tandem with market rates. If you invest in T-bills yourself, the price you'll be quoted may vary according to the amount you want to buy; the more you invest, the better price you'll get. Because a mutual fund can buy these bills in large quantities, an investor can usually get a higher yield by investing in the fund than by buying directly in the market.

These funds also invest in other money market instruments such as chartered bank certificates of deposit, short-term promissory notes issued by major corporations (sometimes referred to as "corporate paper"), and instruments called "bankers acceptances." These are promissory notes issued by corporations and endorsed by a bank which guarantees that the amount of the note will be paid on the date specified. All of these investments are short-term and very liquid. They are also usually issued in denominations of several hundred thousand dollars, so few individual investors would have sufficient capital to invest directly and take advantage of the high interest rates paid on these instruments.

Instead of valuing their funds on a daily basis to arrive at a net asset value per share, money market and savings funds usually price their shares or units at a fixed value—perhaps $1 or $10. The investor's profit comes in the form of income.

Long-term rates of return on these funds again do not reach the dizzy heights of the equity-based funds, but they are a lot safer. For example, Guardian Short Term Money Fund gained 8.1 per cent during 1987 and averaged an annual compound return of 10.7 per cent for the 10 years to the end of 1987. Bolton Tremblay Money Fund gained 8.2 per cent in the year to Dec. 31, 1987, and showed a five-year average annual compound return of 9.3 per cent. CMA Short-term Deposit Fund gained 7.3 per cent in 1987, and averaged 10.9 per cent in the 10-year period to Dec. 31 that year.

Ethical funds

Relatively new on the Canadian scene, these funds may have a mix of common stocks and fixed-income securities although many focus on equities. The distinguishing factor is that the investments are selected according to "ethical" or "socially responsible" criteria. For instance, a fund may decide not to invest in corporations doing business in South Africa or other countries practising racial discrimination, those involved in the manufacture of armaments, tobacco or alcohol, or those with a poor record on labor relations or environmental pollution. Some funds may take a more positive approach, actively supporting companies meeting certain ethical or religious criteria. In all cases, the fund's investment criteria will be spelled out in its prospectus.

Socially responsible investment criteria might appear to limit severely a fund manager's flexibility to select investments. However, the performance record of ethical investment funds operating in the United States compares well with those of conventional growth funds. Few are yet operating in Canada. One of the few, Ethical Growth Fund, managed by VanCity Investment Services Ltd., turned in a creditable 9.4 per cent gain for 1987. The fund is recently established so longer-term performance records are not yet available.

Closed-end investment funds

As we stated earlier, these are far less numerous than open-end mutual funds; there are only about 20 of them in Canada today. And open-end mutuals are the main subject of this book. However, because of certain similarities, the closed-end funds deserve a quick look.

Closed-end funds start by raising capital from the public through offering shares in the same way as any other corporation. That capital is then used to establish a portfolio of investments run by a fund manager. But once established, the investment pool is "closed" so there will generally be no further offerings of shares. Existing shares are thereafter traded on stock exchanges or on the over-the-counter market; if you want to invest, you buy shares (through a broker) from someone else who is willing to sell them.

Unlike units in an open-end mutual fund, which you can always redeem for their net asset value, closed-end funds' shares generally trade at a discount from the NAV. And, of course, a closed-end fund does not have to give its investors their money back on demand. This may give the fund manager a bit more flexibility in placing investments to take advantage of long-term trends. As well, and again unlike open-end mutuals, some closed-end funds are allowed to invest more than 10 per cent of their assets in any one company, and they may also borrow to make investments.

But from the investor's point of view, a closed-end fund is usually far less flexible; getting your money back means finding a buyer for your shares who is willing to pay your price. When stock markets are falling, that may be very hard to do; at such times, the discount from the NAV may increase sharply.

CHAPTER 3

The Mechanics of Mutual Funds

by John Crane, Marlene Davidge, Douglas A. Cannon, Nigel P.J. Johnston

The Investment Funds Institute of Canada (IFIC) uses a colorful ''parable'' to explain the purpose and operation of mutual funds.* In a nutshell, it goes as follows:

A very successful farmer decided that he should become an investor but realized he lacked the necessary time, knowledge and experience. So, he presented himself at the offices of Bull and Bear Limited, Professional Investment Counsel, and asked to see Mr. Bull, the president. Instead, he was taken to a board room where five distinguished gentlemen sat around a long table. After being introduced, the farmer explained that he had come to make a proposition. He had, he said, amassed ''a nice little sum of money'' which he proposed to give to Bull and Bear to invest for him. However, he continued, he wished certain conditions to be met.

''First,'' he said, ''I don't wish to have all my eggs in one basket. Experience has taught me that the only way to farm successfully is to diversify your crops and your livestock.'' He would require Bull and Bear, he explained, to study all sectors

* Adaptation of ''Prudent Farmer'' from the Canadian Investment Funds Course, administered by IFIC.

of the economy, selecting those with the most potential, then to study all the companies in those sectors, again selecting the most promising. He then required a comparison of all companies selected, in order to determine the 60 or 70 best ones.

There was more. "Things can change quickly," the farmer pointed out. He required an ongoing, full-time market study, with changes made in his portfolio where appropriate.

Nor was the study merely a matter of paperwork, since "I have always found that you can acquire a great deal more information by talking to a man face-to-face." In short, he would require Bull and Bear to study the companies first-hand, visiting plants and talking to management.

There was yet more. He would want Bull and Bear to hold the securities and handle all the paperwork. He merely wished to receive his income, an annual statement for tax purposes, other statements—with an auditor's report—showing activity in his portfolio and the results, *and* regular market forecasts.

The farmer wound up to his finale. "You have every right to be paid," he said. "As an incentive to you, and a protection to me, I suggest that you retain as your fee 1.5 per cent per year of whatever my investments are worth. In this way, the more you make for me, the more you will earn for yourselves. At the same time I will be protected in that, percentage-wise, your fee will remain constant."

After thanking the farmer for the compliment of selecting Bull and Bear, Mr. Bull then summarized the proposition:

1. Continuous full-time investment management;
2. Complete responsibility for the administration of all detailed work involved;
3. Preparation of quarterly reports and the submission to a complete annual audit;
4. Calculation and mailing of periodic dividend statements and annual preparation of a statement for income tax purposes;
5. The retention, as annual fee, of an amount equal to 1.5 per cent of the portfolio's market value.

Agreeing that all was understood, Mr. Bull asked, "Now, sir, would you be kind enough to indicate the amount of the responsibility you wish to entrust us with."

"One thousand dollars," the farmer replied.

An awkward silence followed.

Mr. Bull cleared his throat. "As you look around," he ventured, "you will see that there are five of us. Now 1.5 per cent of $1,000.00 amounts to $15, which means that the most we could receive, at the outset at least, for the time and effort that would be required if we were to accept your proposal, would be $3 each. In all fairness and honesty, I doubt that we could readily accept."

However, Mr. Bull added, if the farmer could interest some of his friends and acquaintances in the idea, and thus combining many $1,000 amounts, they might be able to do business.

The farmer saw the merit in Mr. Bull's suggestion. Over the next few weeks, he explained his idea to friends and acquaintances. Many were interested, but he soon realized that on his own he would take a long time to build a sufficient pool of investment capital. Then he had another idea.

He decided to hire others to tell his story and to prepare brochures describing his idea and its potential.

A reasonable man, he once again realized that this would cost money. How was it to be raised? Logically, he decided that the people who were to benefit from this undertaking should be the ones who paid. And how much should they pay? If charges were too high, people wouldn't join in; too low, he would be unable to meet his costs and suffer a heavy personal loss.

The farmer finally decided upon a very simple method of charging. He decided to form a club. Members—those who contributed their money to the pool—would pay a one-time entry fee of an amount not to exceed 9 per cent of the capital they contributed. These fees would cover all the marketing costs. The result? You probably guessed. An investment fund was born.

This story provides a clear description of the purpose and nature of a mutual fund. But in today's highly complex world of income tax considerations and various legislative jurisdictions, the simple mutual fund described above has undergone considerable refinement.

In Chapter 2 we discussed the concept of the mutual fund and looked at the characteristics of different types of funds. To more fully understand the nature of a mutual fund, let's now take a closer look at both its organization and structure.

Organization and structure

Let's begin with an analysis of the two basic forms a mutual fund can take, incorporated or unincorporated. Should a mutual fund choose to incorporate, it will be known as a mutual fund company or corporation, while those that elect to take the unincorporated route will become mutual fund trusts. The two are most easily distinguished by the types of securities they issue to investors. Trusts issue units while companies issue shares.

Mutual fund trusts

Due to the simpler tax treatment afforded mutual fund trusts, some two-thirds of funds in Canada today fall into this category. A mutual fund trust is defined under a trust deed which contains all of the material facts about the fund:

- fund name
- investment objectives and restrictions of the managers
- a listing of the trustees
- method and frequency of fund valuation
- rights of unit holders
- procedures for the distribution of income and capital gains, or losses
- how purchases/redemptions shall be made

The trust issues securities called units to investors proportionately according to the value of their investment in relation to the total value of the trust. Unit is the term used to describe each part of the trust and, as you'll see later, while the owners' rights are different to shareowners', units can be considered synonymous with shares.

All unitholders are entitled to the same rights and privileges, including the right to vote on certain matters affecting the trust. Currently, tax laws generally allow all income and capital gains/losses to flow through to the unitholders as though they had received them directly.

Companies and corporations

While not as common today, companies were originally formed to comply with both federal and provincial legislation which restricted companies from redeeming their own shares. To help get around this restriction, incorporated mutual funds usually had two classes of stock: nonredeemable and a second class freely offered for public sale and redemption.

More recently, however, legislation has been amended to allow redemption on demand by any unitholder, thus eliminating the need for two different classes of stock. The incorporation of a mutual fund is subject to the same statutes governing any other corporation with the exception of the company's share capital.

As with mutual fund trusts, mutual fund companies' shares are sold (redeemed) to the company itself at what is defined as the net asset value per share. Also similarly, a continuous and unlimited number of shares is authorized.

Like shareholders in any public company, all those holding shares in a mutual fund company are entitled to attend the annual meeting and to vote on matters raised there. A mutual fund company's tax position is, however, somewhat different, as we'll see shortly.

Fund Objectives

As we have seen, mutual funds come in all shapes and sizes and offer a wide variety of choices. After you have determined your own personal investment goals, the next step is to undertake a detailed examination of funds that interest you. This brings us to the prospectus.

All mutual funds are required to provide potential investors with a prospectus, as well as the latest annual or semi-annual financial statements. In the prospectus you will find a section on the fund's investment objectives and policies. To judge whether a fund is right for you, it is important to study closely this statement of the purpose of the fund, as well as the disclosure of risk factors and the tax status of the fund's unitholders. Several legislative safeguards exist to protect investors, but it is ultimately the purchaser's responsibility to conduct his or her own investigation. Regulations require the disclosure of all material facts pertaining to a mutual fund, but the responsibility involved in a purchase rests with the investor.

The structure of a mutual fund

Here, we are concerned with three levels of organization: managers, custodians and distributors. You should understand the function and responsibilities of each of them.

Managers

Mutual fund management companies or trustee(s) retain professional investment advisers to look after the portfolio's assets on an ongoing basis. Advisers make buy and sell decisions within the framework of the fund's stated investment objectives while complying with certain investment powers and restrictions.

Additionally, the advisers must operate within limitations and restrictions set by provincial statutes. In part, these may state that the fund:

- may not purchase more than 10 per cent of the net assets of any single issuer of securities;
- may not purchase securities to gain control of their issuer;
- may not purchase securities on margin or sell short;
- may not lend money (except as it may apply in a case of purchasing debt instruments);
- may not trade in any commodity future contract or commodity futures option.

Fund management companies or trustee(s) also undertake to provide complete support services including the production of annual reports, record-keeping, calculation of net asset value and full disclosure of all material facts affecting the fund.

A great deal of latitude is given portfolio advisers, but they in turn are responsible to the trustee(s) or to a board of directors in the case of mutual fund corporations whose members are elected at the fund's annual meeting.

Custodians

The assets comprising the portfolio of a mutual fund are usually held by a trust company or a chartered bank. This custodian is responsible for the collection and disbursement of all monies involved in investor purchases and redemptions, and all income and monies for the purchase and sale of securities made within the portfolio. As well as being charged with the safekeeping of assets, the custodian may function as the registrar and transfer agent for the fund and must maintain complete, up-to-date, accurate records of all the fund unitholders. More frequently this function is the responsibility of the trustee(s) or management company and in some of these cases is contracted to an administrative service company.

As investing increasingly becomes an international activity, arrangements are often made to facilitate the holding of assets outside the jurisdiction of the host country.

Distributors

Distributors represent the sales arm of the mutual fund organization. Provincial legislation, such as the Ontario Securities Act, usually requires that sales personnel be registered with the securities commission of the province in which they operate. Exceptions to this requirement under certain conditions are made in the cases of trust companies and chartered banks which may sell units in their own funds through their branch offices, provided no sales are solicited. (This is no longer true in Ontario and Saskatchewan at the time of publication and it is reasonably anticipated that soon, no person will be able to sell mutual funds without being licensed.)

Distributors' responsibilities include providing potential investors with an up-to-date prospectus and a copy of the most recent annual and semi-annual financial statements and informing the potential investor about the specific objectives of the fund. Distributors must send confirmations of the purchase and sale transactions, income reinvestments and fee deductions to investors, detailing price, date, dollar amount, and units purchased or sold, plus the prospectus which contains a complete accurate description of the fund. They also deal with their clients' enquiries on any and all aspects of the fund.

The pricing mechanism

As we saw in Chapter 2, the number of units or shares your investment will buy, as well as the amount you'll receive if you sell, is governed by the net asset value per share, or NAV. The formula for calculating the NAV, you'll recall, is as follows:

$$\text{Net asset value per share} = \frac{\text{Market value of all securities plus cash on hand less all outstanding liabilities}}{\text{Total number of shares issued and outstanding}}$$

Generally, each security in the portfolio is valued on the basis of its last sale price as at the date of valuation.

In simple terms, the NAV represents the worth an individual share would have if the fund were to liquidate all its investments, collect all its receivables, pay all debts or obligations and distribute what is left to investors equally in proportion to the number of shares held.

NAV must be calculated at least monthly. Funds with more than 50 per cent of their assets in shares must make valuations at least weekly. Today, you'll find that many equity (common share) funds and some income funds are priced daily.

The right of redemption

A mutual fund's prospectus or simplified prospectus outlines the procedures to be followed for redemptions. Just as all funds continuously sell units or shares to the public, so investors have the right to ask for payment for the value of their investment on any valuation date. This payment (redemption) must be made within seven days of the valuation date on which the redemption request was processed.

In certain circumstances, a fund may suspend or defer its investors' right of redemption. However, generally this would happen only if exchanges (either Canadian or foreign) had suspended normal trading on securities making valuation impossible.

By frequently valuing their assets, mutual funds offer a very highly liquid investment. In order to provide this liquidity, mutual funds' portfolio managers maintain sufficient assets in cash or cash equivalents to be able to provide for redemptions, or administrative fees and potential income and capital distributions. (Over and above these amounts, of course, portfolio managers may, from time to time, hold substantial cash reserves as protection against a possible market slide or to take advantage of buying opportunities at lower prices.)

Construction of an equity portfolio

A common mistake often made by non-professional portfolio managers is to look simply for securities that offer the highest growth potential in a very non-systematic way. Professional portfolio managers, while also interested in growth opportunities, of course, bring a disciplined and systematic approach to the task of building a portfolio. In taking a close look at how managers put together equity portfolios, we shall see how they strive to meet the stated objectives of the fund and to provide the performance element that makes one fund more desirable than another.

Diversification

The professional money manager reduces investment risk through the purchase of a large number of securities, a distinct advantage afforded investors through mutual funds. Most equity funds hold anywhere from 40 to over 100 individual securities, thus providing optimum diversification. This spreading of risk is one of the key benefits of mutual funds.

Risk

Risk can be classified as either ''systematic'' or ''unsystematic.'' Systematic risk represents the overall risk of the marketplace and is often referred to as the ''beta'' of a given security. This beta is used to help determine a particular investment's volatility relative to that of the market as a whole; in other words, does its value fluctuate more or less than the percentage change in the stock market itself?

Unsystematic risk is that associated with the security itself; how well does it perform and how healthy are the situation and prospects of the underlying corporation? This is often referred to as a stock's ''alpha''. For example, a company's launch of a new product or its loss of a market may have a direct bearing on the change in price of that company's shares.

Portfolio managers follow a stock's 'beta' and 'alpha' and often use them in constructing an overall portfolio.

The phrase "The higher the risk, the higher the reward," suggests that if you maximize your risk you will reap the highest possible reward. But excessive risk does not ensure excessive returns. Portfolio managers seek to optimize returns for a given, 'measured' rate of risk.

Macroanalysis: the top-down forecast

Using this approach, the professional money manager examines closely all those factors likely to have an impact on financial markets. This approach, known as a capital market analysis, reviews current economic policies, national and international interest-rate trends, issues affecting investment, specific investment categories, individual industries and sectors within the marketplace and, finally, specific stocks available.

This approach is often referred to as a "top-down" analysis of market opportunities. In other words, starting from a broad-based macroanalysis, a portfolio manager draws a forecast of expectations leading down to specific segments of the economy that are likely to prove the strongest.

Microanalysis: the bottom-up approach

Coming at the task from the opposite end, a microanalyst examines individual companies and their prospects and compares them with their chief competitors in order to determine the company that offers the greatest potential for reward.

Using this "bottom-up" approach, managers look closely at relative price earnings or P/E ratios [share price divided by earnings per share] and yields of various companies. The operative word is *relative*. The P/E becomes meaningful only when measured against some benchmark. A manager may compare a current P/E with past values to see if it is above or below "normal." Or he or she may compare the P/E with those of other stocks in the same industry to see if it is lower (indicating that the stock is better priced).

Managers also often use the overall market's (or its index's) P/E to compare with that of an individual stock, to determine how the stock is priced relative to the market as a whole.

Benchmarks

One of the yardsticks professional money managers use when assembling their portfolios is the composition of the stock exchange against which they most often compete. In Canada this yardstick is the Toronto Stock Exchange Composite Index. The TSE 300, as it is commonly known, comprises 300 stocks in 14 groups or indices, each of which is weighted in order to compute overall performance. For example, here is how the 14 indices were weighted as of December 31, 1987:

Index	*Percentage weighting*
Metals and minerals	10.88
Gold and silver	10.24
Oil and gas	8.42
Paper and forest products	3.85
Consumer products	7.55
Industrial products	8.78
Real estate and construction	1.17
Transportation	2.17
Pipelines	3.15
Utilities	11.00
Communications	4.76
Merchandising	4.20
Financial services	16.15
Management companies	7.68

After studying these weightings, the manager then makes adjustments according to his or her reading of the economic climate. For example, a manager studying the above weightings at a time when he or she perceives recession to be imminent might decide to invest only 5.44 per cent of the fund's portfolio (or half the TSE weighting) in metals and minerals, because during a recession metals and minerals stocks tend to perform poorly since the underlying companies' earnings usually decline significantly. The same is true of the paper and forest products sector, so the fund's investment here might be set at only two per cent. On the other hand, utilities stocks tend to hold up well in a recession, so here the fund's portfolio might be overweighted to perhaps 20 per cent.

The 14 indices are broken down into sub-indices (for instance, gas, electrical and telephone are the three utilities sub-indices), and they too are weighted. Again, the manager will work through them and overweight or underweight according to his or her perception of the economic future. Finally, the TSE Index gives weightings to each of the 300 stocks that comprise it, and the manager can use these as well when making purchasing decisions.

In this way, by making a series of decisions to overweight or underweight a given sector or stock, the manager shapes a portfolio which, it is anticipated, will maximize returns and minimize risk.

Construction of a bond portfolio

Portfolio managers of bond funds, as we saw in Chapter 2, have quite different objectives than those of equity fund managers. Their prime task is to maximize income and preserve capital; enhancing capital is a secondary goal. But their approach to building a portfolio is no less disciplined than that of equity fund managers.

The securities these managers select (which may include shorter-term money market instruments as well as medium and long-term bonds), generate a predetermined level of income for a specified time period. The manager takes into account the factors that determine this income level:

a) Prevailing interest rates.
b) The term to maturity. Longer-term bonds normally produce a higher level of income than shorter-term ones.
c) The credit quality of the issuing government or corporation. Bonds issued by the most creditworthy borrowers, such as the Government of Canada, produce lower income levels but are the most secure, while securities issued by corporations and governments with lower credit ratings, yield a higher

return, at least initially. (Over the longer term, sacrificing safety for income will not prove a wise decision if the issuer defaults on interest payments and principal repayments.)

The manager must also take into account capital values. As we have seen, the capital value of marketable fixed-income securities such as bonds and money market instruments is affected by changes in interest-rate levels. Capital values and interest-rate levels move in opposite directions; falling interest rates produce rising prices (and hence capital gains), while rising interest rates cause prices to fall.

The manager also recognizes that term to maturity influences the impact of a change in the level of interest rates. For example, if interest rates fall by one percentage point (i.e., from 10 per cent to 9 per cent), a Treasury bill or bond with a one-year term to maturity will gain almost 1 per cent, a five-year bond will gain 3–4 per cent, while a 20-year bond will gain 8-9 per cent. Capital losses of comparable magnitude occur when interest rates rise.

These factors combine to create a real dilemma for the manager of a bond fund. To obtain the highest possible income level and the greatest stability of income, he or she must purchase bonds with a very long term to maturity. Unfortunately, since longer-term bonds are the biggest losers in a rising interest-rate environment, this strategy will leave the fund most vulnerable to an erosion of capital value if rates do rise unexpectedly.

But if the fund holds a high proportion of very short-term bonds and money market instruments, it is in a poor position if interest rates decline, since when those investments mature the monies must be invested in bonds with lower interest or coupon rates.

Finding a middle ground

To resolve these conflicts, bond fund managers carefully structure their portfolios to meet the requirement for income and capital safety. The first step is to draw up a set of guidelines to ensure that the fund will meet its objective over the longer term. These are the major ones:

- *Define an acceptable range for the average term to maturity of the overall portfolio*. Since long-term bond prices decline most when interest rates rise, the upper limit for term to maturity will be determined by the fund's emphasis on capital preservation. It is important to establish a range: the lower limit on term to maturity ensures that the manager does not significantly reduce the fund's income level by focusing solely on a capital preservation strategy. This term-to-maturity range is frequently six to 12 years.

• *Define guidelines for credit quality.* Conservatively managed bond funds will purchase only government securities and investment-grade corporate securities with a credit rating of A, AA, or AAA because securities with lower ratings have a higher probability of default. (Other guidelines may limit the fund's overall investment in lower-rated corporate securities to further control credit quality.)

• *Establish rules for diversification.* This involves limiting the proportion of fund assets that can be invested in the securities of any single non-government issuer. The usual maximum is 10 per cent, but conservatively-managed funds will frequently stop at 5 per cent to limit default risk and improve marketability.

Once these guidelines have been established, the manager will then carefully consider the interest rate outlook and construct an investment portfolio that best meets the objectives of the fund.

The first step is to purchase a collection of bonds that will make up the income-oriented "core portfolio." This core portfolio normally comprises 50 to 60 per cent of total assets and consists of higher-yielding bonds issued by federal, provincial and municipal governments and by top-quality corporations.

The fund's managers then invest the balance of the assets in more liquid, less income-oriented bonds and money market securities. This portion of the fund reflects the manager's short-term (one to three months) interest-rate outlook.

Many factors determine the composition of this portion of the fund. They include bond supply and demand, exchange-rate movements and seasonal forces that have a short-term impact on interest rates.

This section of the portfolio is also traded actively, moving into longer-term bonds when interest rates are expected to decline, shifting to shorter-term assets when rate rises are expected. Trades are also made to allow the fund to profit from changing relative values. For example, when provincial governments are expected to issue a large supply of new securities, the price of provincial bonds often falls relative to the prices of other types of securities. In this circumstance, the manager might reduce the fund's holding of provincials, hoping to repurchase them at a lower price.

Trading between markets is also used to add value. When the Canadian dollar is expected to fall or the interest-rate differences between Canada and foreign countries is unsustainably low, the fund may benefit from selling Canadian bonds to buy foreign-currency bonds, then reversing the transaction at a later date. In practice, since the yield on Canadian bonds is attractive relative to those available elsewhere in the world, such trades are undertaken only if the expected gain will more than offset the associated reduction of income.

Construction of a balanced portfolio

Portfolio managers of balanced funds, striving for a mix of growth and income, buy both equities and bonds. They must therefore bring to the task of portfolio construction all the approaches both equity and bond fund managers use. Beyond that, they must ensure that the overall portfolio is indeed balanced, with just the right mix of growth and income investments.

Taxation and mutual fund trusts

It's time now to take a look at the tax treatment accorded mutual funds and investors therein. Unless otherwise noted, we are assuming that the investor is an individual resident in Canada for tax purposes.

Since most publicly-offered mutual funds qualify as mutual fund trusts, we are only going to discuss special tax rules to which they are subject. The objective of these rules is to treat the trust merely as a conduit so that, generally speaking, an investor pays tax on his or her returns just as if the investments had been made directly in the fund's underlying assets.

Taxation and mutual fund companies/ corporations

As we've already seen, some mutual funds are structured as companies or corporations. Generally speaking, for certain types of income they do not provide quite the same degree of integration or flow-through as do the trusts. The implications of this for their shareholders, however, are minimal.

Like any public company, a mutual fund company or corporation is required to pay tax on its income. However, when it makes distributions to its shareholders, this tax is fully refundable. The main effect of this, so far as the shareholders are concerned, is that all forms of income which the mutual fund generates are passed on to the shareholder as dividends from a taxable Canadian corporation, and the shareholder can hence take advantage of the dividend tax credit.

This means that the investor whose fund did indeed generate income from investing in taxable Canadian corporations will generally be in exactly the same tax position as if he or she had invested directly in the underlying shares that generated the income.

In the case of other income such as interest and income from foreign sources, the mutual fund company or corporation pays tax at a lower rate before making a distribution. This rate is approximately equal to the tax payable had the investor earned the income directly. So even though the shareholders receive an after-tax amount rather than the entire before-tax amount they would have received if they had invested directly, their final tax position will in most cases be about the same.

As well, mutual fund companies and corporations are allowed to identify separately as "capital gains dividends," income generated by making such gains, and that income in the investor's hands is treated exactly as if he or she had made a direct capital gain in the market.

As with mutual fund trusts, the redemption of shares of a

mutual fund company or corporation may result in a capital gain (or loss), and the above discussion and example concerning the $100,000 lifetime capital gains exemption and cumulative net investment losses is equally applicable to capital gains realized through the sale of shares in this type of mutual fund.

Taxation of a mutual fund trust

Generally speaking, any income of the trust (including capital gains) that is not paid or made payable in the year to unitholders will be subject to tax in the trust. Since a trust pays tax at the highest rate applicable to individuals, the document governing the trust inevitably requires the trustee to cause sufficient income to be paid or payable to the unitholders so that the trust will not be subject to tax. The trust then deducts these amounts when computing its income. The unitholder then declares them as income, no matter whether they have been received in cash or reinvested in additional units.

A mutual fund trust may make certain designations so that the nature of the income which it earns and distributes to unitholders is preserved in the hands of the unitholder. Usually the trustee will make all such designations available; otherwise, unitholders would have to pay tax at the full rate on all income from the fund even though, as we'll now see, some of that income may be eligible for more favorable tax treatment.

Dividends from taxable Canadian corporations

Dividends received from a taxable Canadian corporation earn special tax treatment to reflect the fact that they are paid out of the corporation's after-tax income. Under tax reform, dividends received will be grossed-up by 25 per cent and a dividend tax credit of 13⅓ per cent of the grossed-up dividend is then allowed against federal tax. The net effect is a lower taxation rate; for instance, an Ontario resident paying tax at the new top marginal rate of 43.5 per cent will pay approximately 30 per cent on dividend income in 1988.

Since a mutual fund trust usually designates that the share of income paid or payable in a year to a unitholder includes the unitholder's pro-rata share of dividends received by the trust, the unitholder is entitled to the same favorable tax treatment that would be accorded had the dividends been received directly from the corporation.

Capital gains

The taxable portion of a capital gain (and the allowable portion of a capital loss) has traditionally been 50 per cent. Under tax reform, however, the proportion increases to 66.6 per cent in 1988 and to 75 per cent in 1990. Even with these increases, the tax treatment of capital gains is still favourable; a top-marginal-rate Ontario resident will pay approximately 29.9 per cent on capital gains in 1988 and approximately 33.6 per cent in 1990.

And, of course, he or she may pay nothing at all, since individuals are generally permitted a cumulative lifetime exemption from tax on up to $100,000 of net capital gains.

Again a mutual fund trust usually makes designations to the effect that the unitholder receiving capital gains may take advantage of these rules.

Foreign income

A Canadian resident is liable to Canadian tax on all his or her income, including that from foreign sources. Those earning income from foreign sources are entitled to a foreign tax credit which may, in certain cases, be less than the amount of foreign taxes paid. For example, on foreign property income, the tax credit cannot exceed 15 per cent of the foreign income.

Once again, a mutual fund trust generally makes designations to the effect that foreign income flows through to the unitholder, who will then be taxed in the usual way. There is one proviso: for the purposes of making the designation, the trust will not be considered to have paid foreign tax on income from property at a rate exceeding 15 per cent. This rate is generally equal to the tax rate on property income Canadian residents earn from sources in those countries with which Canada has a comprehensive tax treaty. As a result, the 15 per cent foreign tax credit limitation generally affects only mutual fund trusts investing in non-treaty countries.

Losses

A mutual fund trust may not flow net capital losses or other net losses through to unitholders. Such losses must be carried forward and deducted by the trust in computing income in subsequent years.

In this regard, there is currently an anomaly in the Income Tax Act. As we have seen, a fund's declaration of trust usually requires that all its income be paid or made payable in the year to unitholders because it can then deduct that income and hence pay no tax. However, if the trust has distributed all of its income and capital gains, it will never be able to use its net capital losses or other net losses carried forward from prior years.

To correct this anomaly an amendment to the Income Tax Act has been proposed. Under the amendment, a trust will be permitted when computing its income to deduct less than the full amount of income paid or payable to unitholders. Only the amount deducted by the trust will be included in the income of unitholders even though they have received a larger amount.

Dispositions of shares or units

When a fundholder redeems an investment in a mutual fund, he or she will realize a capital gain (or loss) to the extent that the proceeds of disposition, net of disposition costs, are more (or less) than the adjusted cost base (cost value) of the shares or units (see below).

A disposition also occurs when shares or units are transferred to an RRSP or are exchanged for shares or units of another fund. There is also a deemed disposition on the death of a fundholder.

The adjusted cost base of units at any time is generally the amount paid for the units plus the amount of any distributions reinvested in additional units. If a fund has sustained losses and has elected not to deduct the full amount of income distributed to unitholders in the manner described above, the adjusted cost base will be reduced by the portion of distributions received that are not included in income.

As noted above, a unitholder will be required to include the taxable portion of a capital gain in the computation of his income, although no tax may be paid if the individual has not yet used up the lifetime capital gains exemption of $100,000. However, under tax reform, the amount of taxable capital gains eligible for the lifetime exemption in any year will be reduced by the individual's "cumulative net investment loss" claimed after 1987. So far as a mutual fund investment is concerned, this "net investment loss" will, generally speaking, be the investment interest expense less "passive" income including interest and grossed-up dividends. The following example illustrates the effect of these new rules:

An investor borrows $10,000 on January 1, 1988 at 12 per cent interest to purchase 1,000 units of a mutual fund trust. In 1988, he receives $480 of income from the trust, in the form of dividends from taxable Canadian corporations. The individual reinvests the distribution in 40 additional units. On December 31, 1988, he sells the 1,040 units for $12,000 and repays the loan. The tax consequences of the disposition would be as follows:

Proceeds of disposition	$12,000
Adjusted cost base	$10,480
Capital gain	$ 1,520
Taxable capital gain (66.6 per cent)	$ 1,013

Investment expense—interest on loan	$ 1,200
Investment income—grossed-up dividends (25 per cent gross-up)	$ 600
Cumulative net investment loss	$ 600
Taxable capital gain	$ 1,013
Less: Cumulative net investment loss	$ 600
Taxable capital gain eligible for capital gains exemption	$ 413
Non-eligible taxable capital gain	$ 600

The taxpayer has a $600 taxable capital gain which is not sheltered by the $100,000 lifetime capital gains exemption, but this gain can be offset by the $600 net investment loss, so that no tax is payable. However, due to the new "cumulative net investment loss'' rule proposed under tax reform, the taxpayer cannot then use the $600 net investment loss to offset other income. Before the introduction of this rule, the full $1,013 taxable capital gain could have been sheltered with the lifetime capital gains exemption so that the $600 net investment loss could have been used to offset other income.

CHAPTER 4

How to Read Mutual Fund Prospectuses and Financial Statements

by John Grundy

It's a frosty Friday in February, a few days before the cutoff date for RRSP contributions. You have been presented with a prospectus, assorted statements and other material by the salesperson opposite you. All it takes now to buy a mutual fund is your signature.

But what is a prospectus? And what are all these other statements? The glossy picture of the couple lounging at poolside sure is appealing. Maybe you'll read this material later, just as everyone else does. Don't they?

Hold on a minute. Why are you buying this particular fund? Because you liked the ads? Because a friend of your brother said it was a good deal tax-wise?

By now, more questions than answers should be forming in your mind about this investment. And it's very important for both your future peace of mind and your future financial situation that you understand thoroughly the nature of this fund and how it operates. That information, together with other important details, is in the prospectus.

A prospectus is a legal disclosure document. It contains the rights and obligations of who may do what, when, how and to whom. The name is derived from the Latin verb "to look"—and you really should have a thorough look before buying into the fund.

Every organization offering mutual funds for sale to the public must, by provincial law, file a prospectus with the securities commission in whose jurisdiction sales are targeted. National and provincial policy statements, within the context of the various securities acts, dictate which requirements must be met in the creation, distribution and operation of mutual funds. The provincial regulations do not in any way assess the relative merits of a particular fund and a statement to that effect is contained on the front page of all prospectuses.

Two filing options are available to mutual fund organizers: the prospectus system and the simplified prospectus system.

Under the prospectus system, the document must present information concerning the organization and its objectives, specific details of the fund, its manner of operation and audited financial statements. A simplified prospectus contains less detail and uses less complex wording. However, a participant in a fund, using the simplified prospectus system is also entitled to receive on request the fund's latest audited financial statements, a list of portfolio holdings and portfolio transactions and copies of all documents in what is known as the fund's permanent information record.

The key document in this permanent information record is the annual information form. This covers both the information in the simplified prospectus and additional facts required by securities legislation to be disclosed. The record also includes all other documents filed with regulatory authorities by the fund. These might include information circulars relating to shareholders' meetings, press releases about material changes made in the fund's operation and annual filings made in lieu of annual meetings.

In a standard prospectus the main features of a fund's operation are usually summarized at the outset. That summary should never be accepted as an adequate basis on which to make an investment decision. It is crucial to digest the more detailed information in the body of the document (or, in the case of a simplified prospectus, in the permanent information record), to appreciate fully what you're getting into.

It is sometimes said that both the prospectus system and the simplified prospectus system with its back-up documentation are altogether too much of a good thing, that they provide too much information. True, much of the content of a prospectus, and much of its language, may at first intimidate the uninitiated. Nonetheless, the prospectus *should* be read—and some sections studied closely—in order to get a clear picture of just where your after-tax investment dollas are going. Let us, then, "walk" through the various sections of a typical prospectus to see what they reveal.

Investment Objectives and Policies

This is the name usually given to one of the most important sections in a prospectus. As you know already, the fund's investment objectives should match your investment needs: a bond fund is not the place for your dollars if you want capital gains. Chapter 1 showed you how to take a rough measurement of your own tolerance for risk, while Chapters 2 and 3 discussed the levels of risk associated with different kinds of funds. Now, a careful consideration of the Objectives and Policies section of the prospectus will tell you if this specific fund delivers the kind of investment you need, no more and no less.

Management of the fund

This section of the prospectus details who is responsible for the general management of the fund and its assets. The managers may or may not be the same group who will make the detailed investment decisions. If the portfolio is managed by a separate organization, it is the fund manager's job to ensure that that organization is adequately fulfilling the fund's investment objectives.

The prospectus section dealing with portfolio management briefly describes the manager's history and details the amount and types of other assets under the same management. (Although some portfolio management teams are created with the sole purpose of managing a specific fund—and do so competently—many investors feel more at ease knowing that their investments are being directed by people with a broader record of business success.) There will also usually be an outline of the manager's investment philosophy. Overall, this section provides a means of gauging the important sense of compatibility that should exist between the fund's operators and its shareholders.

Investment restrictions

Here, you find out what kinds of activities this fund will avoid. You'll learn, for instance, whether it is permitted to put more than 10 per cent of it's asset into foreign investments, and whether short sales or purchases on margin are permitted. Here is more information that will help you to decide if the potential investment activities of the fund are compatible with your goals.

Full details of a fund's investment restrictions are usually not set out in a simplified prospectus. If a fund uses a simplified prospectus, the potential investor may want to study the permanent information record to discover any restrictions.

Fees

The fees charged by a fund are a very important consideration for the potential buyer. Until a few years ago, the costs to the investor were fairly straightforward in the case of most funds. Today, the subject of fees has become complex—indeed, Chapter 8 of this book is devoted exclusively to fees and other charges—and some incidental expenses may be overlooked if your examination of the prospectus (and possibly the permanent information record) is less than thorough—not least because details of the fees are scattered here and there throughout the prospectus. In spite of periodic calls for provincial authorities to regulate that all fees and expenses be shown in one section, the prospective buyer must still work through several sections for the full story concerning the monies that will be charged against his or her investment. They may include front-end and back-end loads, distribution fees, transfer fees and fees for "custom" services. They will certainly include management fees, a charge common to all funds. *Somewhere* in the prospectus, all the information will be there. Government regulators do a good job of ensuring that full disclosure of all potential charges is made in the prospectus — and also, incidentally, of ensuring that those charges are not unreasonably high compared to those of comparable financial services.

Distribution of income

There is information on how the fund's income is distributed, whether it is paid in cash or reinvested in additional units, and on the tax implications for participants, usually with a notation that a legal opinion has been obtained. (Because individuals' tax situations vary, it may be wise for potential investors to seek professional advice before investing in a particular fund.)

Sale of shares

A section of the prospectus outlines how the fund's shares will be distributed. It names those authorized to make sales to the public, and specifies what sales incentives may be used, as well as minimum purchase size.

In this section we find the actual price at which an investment can be made. We may also find some information on fees; funds with front-end loads here set out load levels and any details of sliding scales whereby the charge declines as larger purchases are made.

The section also outlines various purchase options that may be available, such as a periodic payment plan that allows an investor to acquire an increasing interest in a fund on a budgeted basis.

Systematic withdrawal options may also be described here. Such plans are particularly useful for a retirement-age investor who needs income but doesn't want to pull entirely out of a fund. Systematic withdrawal plans are discussed in detail in Chapter 9.

Redemption procedures

An important aspect of any open-ended mutual fund is the procedure involved when an investor wishes to redeem shares. All funds must describe their specific redemption procedures in the prospectus, and also disclose circumstances under which they may withhold the right of immediate redemption.

As we already saw in Chapter 3, securities commissions' regulations require that funds pay the proceeds from redemptions within seven business days of the valuation date on which they were processed. This statement will therefore be common to all prospectuses.

In some prospectuses, this is where more information about fees will appear, such as the costs that may be involved for fundholders wishing to sell.

Details of the circumstances under which the routine redemption of shares can be suspended should be studied closely. Most commonly this is allowed if the fund is temporarily unable to sell underlying assets to raise the cash needed. Another reasonable cause to temporarily suspend redemptions is mentioned in Chapter 3 — the unlikely event that more than 50 per cent of the fund's assets have been suspended from trading by market authorities.

Legal disputes

The prospectus must also make note of any outstanding legal disputes that may affect the status of the fund. It is rare for Canadian mutual funds to become embroiled in legal proceedings. But if one does, it is probably wise to look for another fund with equally attractive investment objectives—and without the shadow of potentially costly and disruptive legal actions. If the fund's attractions can't be matched, the prospective investor should at least get more details of those actions from the fund's manager.

Risk factors

All prospectuses contain a section entitled Risk Factors, setting out in general terms the nature of the risks facing an investor who purchases the fund. No matter how obvious those risk factors may seem, it is a useful exercise to read this section slowly. Out loud. Several times.

Rights of rescission

All securities commissions' regulations allow buyers the right to rescind a purchase agreement within 48 hours of having received a prospectus and any other legally required documentation. This right to rescind a decision is outlined in all prospectuses, usually near the end of the document, just before the financial statements.

The right of rescission exists to protect investors who have second thoughts about the suitability to them of the purchase, perhaps in response to a smooth but less than well-intentioned sales presentation. The buyer who exercises this right may not get all the investment back. If the value of the funds or units has dropped in those 48 hours, the fund is required to return only that lower current value. However, if the buyer paid a front-end load, this must be reimbursed in full.

With this right goes the responsibility of understanding what is being bought. This can only be achieved by reading the prospectus and getting clarification of those sections that are not clearly understood.

Financial statements

Issuers of mutual funds are required to provide prospective investors with details of the overall financial condition of the fund. This financial information appears at the end of the prospectus or, if the fund uses the simplified prospectus, is detailed in separate reports that also contain details of the securities held and other assets of the fund.

The financial section includes an auditor's report or if the statements are for a period that does not reflect the fund's fiscal year-end, a declaration to the effect that the figures are unaudited.

The auditor's report is usually a two-paragraph affair. The first identifies what organization was audited, for what period, whether the audit was conducted under accepted procedures and the scope of the examinations. The second is the auditor's professional opinion.

The opinion paragraph outlines whether the statements show

fair and consistent representation of the financial condition of the fund. If they do, that is noted and the auditor's statement is considered to be an "unqualified" opinion. Statements accompanied by a qualified opinion usually contain the words "except for" and may be a warning to investors that some aspect of the fund's financial position may not be in accordance with generally accepted standards of operation.

The financial reports consist of a balance sheet, statements of income and retained earnings, a statement of changes in financial position and a statement of portfolio holdings. Together, they present a complete story of all important aspects of the fund's operations and must be clearly understood by the potential buyer wanting to know how his or her investments will be managed.

The balance sheet usually appears first. It shows the financial condition of the fund at a specific date, usually the fund's fiscal year-end. (Fiscal year-ends do not necessarily coincide with calendar year-ends.) In quarterly or semi-annual reports the specific date will be the end of the period reported on. It covers three distinct areas: assets, liabilities and shareholders' equity. Assets comprise what the fund owns, liabilities comprise what is owed and shareholders' equity is what's left over. Shareholders' equity can be referred to as financial net worth.

Typically appearing on the asset side of the balance sheet are: cash and cash equivalents such as money market investments, subscription receivables, other receivables such as accrued interest, dividends and other amounts owed to the fund, recoverable and deferred tax payments and, of course, the fund's prime asset, the value of its investment portfolio. These investments are shown at their market value and represent a type of inventory, being the source of profits yielded by the investment management activity.

The opposite side of the balance sheet shows the fund's liabilities and shareholders' equity. Liabilities consist of amounts due to brokers for transactions contracted but not paid for, amounts payable to shareholders who are redeeming their fund shares and fees payable for such items as investment management, taxes and general administration.

Deducting total liabilities from total assets yields both shareholders' equity and aggregate net asset value of the fund. This, when divided by the number of shares outstanding, produces the net asset value per share.

Shareholders' equity is made up of the original dollar amounts invested in the fund by the buyers, the original dollar value of any other class of shares outstanding, retained earnings and unrealized appreciation in the value of the investments (the difference between cost and market value).

Because open-ended mutual funds give fundholders the right to immediate redemption of their investments, most funds maintain fairly substantial assets in the form of cash and marketable short-term securities. No specific percentage can be cited as necessarily desirable or undesirable; much of the cash and equivalents held simply reflects the fund manager's guesstimate of redemption activities. In part, it also reflects the manager's strategic assessment of a desirable level of liquidity for future investment opportunities. The percentage, known as the "liquidity ratio", can easily be determined by dividing total assets into the total of cash and cash equivalents.

Since the recent explosive growth of mutual funds in North America, some analysts keep a watchful eye on this cash component as a barometer of future market behavior. Holding too much cash in rising markets or too little in falling ones can mean lost opportunities.

The second financial statement shown is usually that of income and expense. It summarizes cash inflow and outflow. Depending upon the type of fund, income outflows may be shown simply as dividends and interest. Investment management fees and any applicable taxes are expenses charged against the inflow. The balance is net investment income. This, when divided by the average number of shares outstanding during the reporting period, shows net investment income per share.

Also given is data on the distribution and composition of earnings to the shareholders on a per-share basis. Dividing this figure by the net asset value per share produces a percentage yield factor; this can then be used to compare the yield of the fund against similar funds or against a market index.

Usually, the balance sheet and income statements have footnote references which more fully explain the statistics shown. A discussion of the fund's management fee structure is often presented in this way.

The statement of retained earnings provides the link between the income statement and the balance sheet. Usually shown first are the accumulated earnings from prior periods. Income for the current period, including capital gains and losses, is added. Then the year's dividend distribution is deducted. Changes in investments' market values are also shown, resulting in a new figure for appreciation of investment value. The new balance at the end of the period shows how the retained earnings either rose or fell compared to the prior period.

The statement of changes in the financial position statement details the sources and uses of funds which provided the net asset value figure for the period under review. To the prior period's net asset value are added (a) the dollar proceeds of new unit sales, (b) dividend reinvestments, (c) the current period's net investment income, (d) the change in investments' market value and (e) gains or losses on sales of securities. From the resultant figure, the total of redemptions and dividend outflows from the fund during the period are deducted. The final figure represents the net asset value at the end of the period.

Many financial statements include a listing of investments held at the end of the period, and a summary of portfolio transactions is readily available from the fund sponsor. The list of securities held, which also shows their percentage of the total portfolio, can indicate whether the fund's objectives are being pursued as planned.

Many investors may not be able to judge the merits of each individual investment held. But a grasp of the overall portfolio structure and information in the financial statements will reveal the course the fund is on. Along with the rest of the material in the prospectus (or that supporting a simplified prospectus), this is the information you need to determine if this mutual fund will meet your specific needs. Read. Now. Before you sign.

CHAPTER 5

Mutual Funds: Bulls and Bears

by Eric Kirzner

Our Canadian economy is subject to sudden and vicious change. As an example, let's examine the events of the past two decades. During this period we have had four recessions: February-September 1970, June 1974-March 1975, November 1979-June 1980, and July 1981-December 1982, the last being one of the most severe on record. We experienced one period of excessive inflation from 1973–1982, when prices more than doubled and rose at an annual compound rate of 9.7 per cent. 1979–1982 was a time of astronomically high interest rates when 91-day Treasury bill yields averaged 15.39 per cent. And we lived through the stock market crash of October 1987 which in terms of percentage decline was the most dramatic since 1914. The severity of these events was unpredictable, and such changes have widespread and often adverse effects on investment portfolios.

During periods of economic growth, common shares and hence equity mutual funds usually show high returns. During recessions, common shares go into a tailspin. On the other hand, as interest rates decline during a recession, fixed-income securities (bond and mortgage funds) perform well. As rates rise at the later stages of economic growth, bond and mortgage funds become depressed in price.

Inflation has become a fact of life in this century and also has major consequences for investment portfolios. Over the past 60 years, prices measured by the consumer price index (CPI) have risen in 51 years and fallen in only nine. In fact, the last year of deflation was 1952! Economists argue that a rising price level of about 3 per cent per year is reasonably healthy and sustainable. But when it rises more steeply there are large and often disparate redistribution effects.

Canadians who suffer most in inflationary periods are those on fixed incomes, primarily elderly, retired people who watch helplessly as the purchasing power of their hard-earned savings shrinks away. As high inflation normally results in rising interest rates, people who have invested all their assets in long term bond funds miss out on the higher income levels that rising rates provide.

During periods of moderate inflation, equity mutual funds normally provide solid investment returns. But if inflation escalates to excessive levels, equity funds may stagnate. This happened in the 1946–1947 post-war period, in the middle 1970's and in late 1980–1981, when inflation peaked at over 12.5 per cent in Canada. When high inflation eventually gives way to low inflation, interest rates drop and bond funds may show large returns.

As an example of the effect inflation can have on investment returns, consider the five-year period from the beginning of 1972 to the end of 1976, when Canadian common stocks as measured by the Toronto Stock Exchange 300 Composite Index, returned a modest 4.47 per cent annual compound rate of return. In a nutshell, not spectacular. However over this same period the CPI rose by an average of 8.4 per cent per annum. Investors in fact lost almost 4 per cent per year in purchasing power with common stock investments.

This is not to suggest that common stocks are a poor investment in today's inflationary world. In fact, you will soon see that equity investments have provided a good hedge against inflation *over the long term*. The point to be made is the importance of measuring returns to reflect the effects of inflation. (Incidentally, economists refer to the unadjusted return of 4.47 per cent as nominal return while the −4 per cent is an inflation-adjusted or real return.)

Later in this chapter you will learn of proven methods of disaster-proofing your mutual fund investments to protect your hard-earned savings and hence your financial future against unwelcome economic shocks and surprises.

Bull and bear markets . . . what they are, what to do

As you probably know, when we have a rising and active stock market, we have a bull market, while a falling market is a bear market. Bulls are typically more frequent than bears, and of longer duration. But bears are vicious. Table 1 shows what happened in the six major bear markets since 1928. Share prices fell by an average of 25 per cent, and the nominal and real (or price-adjusted) value of a $1,000 investment fell to $747.03 and $706.55 respectively. This means you would have needed a subsequent increase in share prices of 33.3 per cent just to recoup your losses! (If a security price falls by 25 per cent, say from $100 to $75, it takes a 33.3 per cent increase to get back, in this case to 100.) Table 1 also shows how Government of Canada bonds outperformed stocks during these bear markets, both on yield, and in nominal and real value changes.

However, it's encouraging — and important — to note how quickly stock prices generally recover from the ravages of bear markets. In Table 2, you'll see that, with the exception of the monster 1929–32 crash, stock prices have recovered their bear-market losses within one to three years in nominal terms and their full purchasing power in two to five years.

Table 3 shows longer term rates of return achieved by Canadian common stocks. These returns would have been achieved by investors who held common stocks through both the many bull and bear markets experienced over the past 25 years.

These tables tell you two things. First, if you are a patient and truly long term investor, you can wait out the storm and earn your returns. For the ten years ending December 31st, 1987, the Canadian Stock Market as measured by the T.S.E. 300

TABLE 1 *Canadian Bear Markets 1924–1987*

Period	*Return on Common Shares, %*	*Nominal value of $1,000 Investment*	*Real Value of $1,000 Investment*	*Government of Canada Bond Returns %*	*Nominal Value of $1,000 Investment*	*Real Value of $1,000 Investment*
1929–32	−64.34	$356.60	$443.30	19.40	$1,194.00	$1,484.30
1937–40	−26.28	737.20	657.50	10.74	1,107.40	987.68
1957	−20.58	794.20	778.30	6.40	1,064.00	1,042.70
1969–70	− 4.40	956.00	900.20	19.16	1,191.60	1,122.05
1974	−25.93	740.70	659.40	−1.69	983.10	875.19
1981	−10.25	897.50	800.60	−3.02	969.80	865.09
Average	−25.30	$747.03	$706.55	8.50	$1,084.98	$1,062.83

Source: Phelim P. Boyle, Harry. H. Panjer, Keith P. Sharp, *Report On Canadian Economic Statistics, 1924–1986*, Canadian Institute of Actuaries, June 1987.

TABLE 2 *Bear Market Recoveries, 1924–1987*

Period	*Return on Common Shares, %*	*Nominal value of $1,000 Investment*	*Real Value of $1,000 Investment*	*Year of Full Nominal Recovery*	*Year of Full Real Recovery*
1929–32	−64.34	$356.60	$443.30	1945	1943
1937–40	−26.28	737.20	657.50	1942	1945
1957	−20.58	794.20	778.30	1958	1959
1969–70	−4.4	956.00	900.20	1971	1972
1974	−25.93	740.70	659.40	1977	1979
1981	−10.25	897.50	800.60	1983	1983
Average	−25.30	$747.03	$706.55		

Source: Phelim P. Boyle, Harry H. Panjar, Keith P. Sharp, *Report On Canadian Economic Statistics, 1924–1986*, Canadian Institute of Actuaries, June 1987.

TABLE 3 Total Rates of Return on Canadian Common Stocks For Periods Ending December 31st, 1987

	Annualized Percentage Change						
T.S.E.	*1 yr*	*3 yr*	*5 yr*	*10 yr*	*15 yr*	*20 yr*	*25 yr*
(Dividends Reinvested)	5.88	13.00	13.79	16.01	10.99	10.74	10.83
Canadian C.P.I.	4.15	4.22	4.25	7.12	7.84	6.87	6.06

Source: The Canadian Performance Monitor, Merrill Lynch Canada Inc.

Index returned 16.01 per cent per annum, well in excess of the average inflation rate of 7.12 per cent. For the past twenty-five years the T.S.E. 300 returned 10.83 per cent per annum, again considerably higher than the 6.06 per cent average inflation rate. Second, these returns could have been increased by timing market turns. However, this is no mean feat. Studies have shown that few professional managers have been able to time the market successfully. Many of them, in fact, willingly admit that they don't even try! They look for undervalued securities, and they hold them through the good times and the bad.

However, if you have the time, inclination and fortitude, there are some valuable guidelines to use for market timing.

Stock market declines normally precede economic slowdowns. So in order to anticipate a bear market, you have to predict economic slumps. And to predict any economic movements, you have to evaluate the economy-wide level of consumer confidence, corporate spending plans, retail spending, homebuilding activity, degree of investor optimism, level of corporate profitability and a host of other important measures. Major bull and bear markets precede turns in the economy by six to 12 months; the average is 11 months. Therefore you need to forecast more than a year ahead.

The most important items to watch are the direction and magnitude of the leading indicators of economic activity. A deterioration in these variables points to economic slow-down, which will be manifested in stagnant or declining gross national product (GNP), the measure of a country's level of economic activity.

So which are the leading indicators? Statistics Canada publishes the Canadian Composite Leading Index which tracks the following 10 indicators:

1. Average work week for manufacturing
2. Residential construction index
3. The U.S. Composite Leading Index
4. New orders for durable goods
5. Shipment-to-inventory ratio for finished goods
6. Price-to-unit labor costs
7. Real money supply
8. Retail trade in furniture and appliances
9. Retail trade in motor vehicles
10. Toronto Stock Exchange 300 Composite Index

If the leading indicator index is negative for several months, particularly in a time of rising unemployment, then there are signs of economic slowdown in the near future and the possibility that the equity market will soon decay. Three of these leading key indicators in particular, the number of hours in the average work week, home-building activity and durable goods orders, generally turn down several months before bear markets.

There are other corraborative factors to look for: interest rates generally trending up, declining retail spending and general lack of consumer and business confidence. As the economic indicators turn down, the equity markets may still appear strong. But history shows that the equity market should start to decline well before the economic slump actually materializes.

Mutual fund performance in bull and bear markets

As we have now seen, stock markets generally fall before and during economic slowdowns. During bear markets, domestic and international equity mutual funds and balanced mutual funds perform poorly. So normally do precious metal funds. Interestingly enough, bond and mortgage funds are also initially hurt in bear markets as the rising interest rates that accompany economic weakness dampen bond prices. The safe harbor is money market funds; they start to yield high returns, normally in both nominal and real dollars.

However, as the bear market intensifies, reflecting recessionary pressures, interest rates start to decline as economic activity abates, so bond funds start to recover. These movements are clearly evident in Table 4 which shows the performance of Canadian equity, international equity, fixed-income and gold funds over the 1980–87 period.

TABLE 4 Mutual Fund Performance, 1980–1987

Year (12 months ended June 30th)	*Equity Funds, %*	*International Equity Funds, %*	*Fixed-Income Funds, %*	*Gold Funds, %*
1980	23.2	13.5	5.7	124.9
1981	20.2	33.5	0.4	-21.5
1982	-26.5	-8.1	13.9	-31.1
1983	65.1	49.1	27.1	95.1
1984	-5.0	-0.1	4.6	-3.7
1985	24.0	21.7	22.1	-8.8
1986	21.0	33.2	14.7	12.7
1987	18.0	18.6	7.4	46.3

Source: *Survey of Funds*, June 30, 1987, The Financial Post Information Service, Maclean Hunter Limited.

As you can see in this table, the high interest rates prevailing in 1981 depressed bond fund yields as we moved into the severe recession that began that July and lasted until December 1982. Equity funds suffered severe losses in 1982 just as the fixed-income funds were starting to recover. Precious metal funds were also depressed and suffered huge losses as high interest rates, reduced inflation expectations and a recessionary environment propelled gold and silver prices downward. Meanwhile, the high yields on Treasury bills spelled dramatic rates of returns for money market funds. But in the 1983 recovery—and the start of a new bull market—equity, bond and precious metal funds showed high returns while money market returns began to diminish.

How then should you react to these economic cycles? There are two strategies, passive and active. The passive approach is an extension of the buy-and-hold strategy outlined below. Don't be misled by the term passive; it doesn't mean that you ignore everything around you! It simply refers to a defensive approach taken regardless of economic cycle forecasts.

Mutual fund investment strategies

The passive approach

Here, you select a mutual fund (or, more appropriately a portfolio of mutual funds), consistent with your financial objectives, and just hold it until retirement, or whatever investment horizon you may have. This is called a simple buy-and-hold strategy and if you choose analytically, using the methods you'll learn in Chapter 6, you should do well in the long run.

As a dramatic illustration, if you had invested in a representative Canadian equity portfolio in 1924 and had simply held on, by 1986 you would have turned a $1,000 investment into $404,230.78! On a more sobering note, this translates into $56,046 in terms of 1986 purchasing power relative to that of 1924, or a 6.6 per cent annual increase in purchasing power before taxes, or roughly 5.9 per cent after tax. You would have had some rocky times along the way, suffering through the 1929–32 bear market (at which point your $1000 investment would have fallen as low as $1,224 from a $3,400 high), the 1937 market break, the recessions of 1939–40, 1957 and 1962 and the savage 1974 bear market. However, you would have been well rewarded for your patience.

You wouldn't have done nearly so well with Government of Canada long-term bonds; over the same period, a $1,000 investment would have grown to $21,347. That's only $2,960 in purchasing power equivalents or a mere 1.7 per cent annual rate of increase before taxes and 0.8 to 1.0 per cent after tax.

All of the foregoing assumes that you were able to buy and hold. If your investment horizon had been shorter, or if you had had to sell at a disadvantageous time, what would have happened? The answer lies in Table 5 which shows annual bond and stock returns, the value of a $1,000 investment and changes in the CPI throughout the period.

TABLE 5 Returns on Bonds and Common Shares, and Changes in the Consumer Price Index, 1924–1986

Year	Government Of Canada Bond Returns (% Change)	Value of $1,000 Investment	Return On Common Shares (% Change)	Value of $1,000 Investment	Consumer Price Index (% Change)
1924	7.84	$ 1,078.40	11.25	$ 1,112.50	−2.14
1925	5.17	1,134.15	28.74	1,432.23	2.73
1926	5.39	1,195.28	24.42	1,781.98	−1.60
1927	10.18	1,316.96	44.92	2,582.45	−1.08
1928	0.56	1,324.34	32.92	3,432.59	0.55
1929	2.34	1,355.33	−11.6	3,034.41	2.72
1930	9.26	1,480.83	−30.9	2,096.78	−5.82
1931	−4.97	1,407.23	−32.96	1,405.68	−10.11
1932	12.37	1,581.31	−12.92	1,224.07	−8.13
1933	7.37	1,697.85	51.63	1,856.05	−2.04
1934	19.66	2,031.65	19.99	2,227.08	1.39
1935	0.83	2,048.51	0.3	2,233.76	2.05
1936	11.12	2,276.31	25.77	2,809.40	1.34
1937	−0.58	2,263.10	−15.34	2,378.44	3.97
1938	5.63	2,390.52	7.8	2,563.95	−1.91
1939	−2.98	2,319.28	−0.23	2,558.06	2.60
1940	8.69	2,520.83	−19.03	2,071.26	4.43
1941	3.8	2,616.62	2.87	2,130.70	6.67
1942	3.08	2,697.21	13.75	2,423.68	3.41
1943	3.88	2,801.86	19.02	2,884.66	1.10

TABLE 5 Returns on Bonds and Common Shares, and Changes in the Consumer Price Index, 1924–1986 — continued

1944	3.16	2,890.40	13.25	3,266.88	−1.09
1945	5.18	3,040.12	35.66	4,431.84	1.10
1946	6.02	3,223.14	−1.51	4,364.92	5.98
1947	3.17	3,325.31	0.79	4,399.41	14.87
1948	−2.38	3,246.17	12.24	4,937.89	8.48
1949	4.85	3,403.61	23.86	6,116.08	1.23
1950	−0.12	3,399.52	51.69	9,277.48	6.1
1951	−3.13	3,293.12	25.44	11,637.67	10.73
1952	1.99	3,358.65	0.01	11,638.83	−1.73
1953	3.64	3,480.91	2.56	11,936.78	0
1954	9.99	3,828.65	39.37	16,636.29	0.35
1955	−0.34	3,815.63	27.67	21,239.56	0.35
1956	−3.63	3,677.12	12.68	23,932.73	3.15
1957	6.4	3,912.46	−20.58	19,007.38	2.03
1958	−5.98	3,678.49	31.25	24,947.18	2.66
1959	−4.67	3,506.71	4.59	26,092.26	1.29
1960	7.1	3,755.68	1.78	26,556.70	1.28
1961	9.78	4,122.99	32.75	35,254.02	0.32
1962	3.05	4,248.74	−7.09	32,754.51	1.57
1963	4.6	4,444.18	15.6	37,864.21	1.86
1964	6.59	4,737.06	25.43	47,493.08	1.82
1965	0.96	4,782.53	6.68	50,665.62	2.99
1966	1.55	4,856.66	−7.07	47,083.56	3.48

1967	−2.2	4,749.81	18.09	55,600.98	4.2
1968	−0.52	4,725.12	22.45	68,083.40	4.03
1969	−2.31	4,615.97	−0.81	67,531.92	4.65
1970	21.98	5,630.55	−3.57	65,121.03	1.48
1971	11.55	6,280.88	8.01	70,337.22	4.87
1972	1.11	6,350.60	27.38	89,595.56	5.1
1973	1.71	6,459.20	0.27	89,837.47	9.27
1974	−1.69	6,350.04	−25.93	66,542.61	12.32
1975	2.82	6,529.11	18.48	78,839.68	9.53
1976	19.02	7,770.94	11.02	87,527.82	5.91
1977	5.97	8,234.87	10.71	96,902.05	9.46
1978	1.29	8,341.10	29.72	125,701.34	8.36
1979	−2.62	8,122.56	44.77	181,977.82	9.8
1980	2.06	8,289.89	30.13	236,807.74	11.19
1981	−3.02	8,039.53	−10.25	212,534.95	12.1
1982	42.98	11,494.92	5.54	224,309.39	9.26
1983	9.6	12,598.43	35.49	303,916.79	4.55
1984	15.09	14,499.54	−2.39	296,653.17	3.76
1985	25.26	18,162.12	25.07	371,024.13	4.35
1986	17.54	21,347.76	8.95	404,230.78	4.17
Real value, 1986		$2,959.83		$ 56,045.92	
Growth rate in real value		1.76%		6.70%	

Source: Phelim P. Boyle, Harry H. Panjer, Keith P. Sharp, *Report on Canadian Economic Statistics, 1924–1986*, Canadian Institute of Actuaries, June 1987.

The active approach

The active approach involves timing, trying to outguess economic swings, buying low and selling high, or revising your portfolio to capture bond market lows and stock market highs. An investor who, during all those years from 1924 to 1986, successfully switched out of stocks into bonds just prior to the bear markets and back into stocks as the bear bottomed out would have turned $1,000 into $6,675,535 for a growth rate of 15.0 per cent per year! Of course, no investor, professional or amateur has a crystal ball for forecasting the future and for picking these moves. But this certainly underscores the value of timing for those who have the time, the expertise and the inclination.

In general, we do not favor the timing approach for non-experts. Studies have shown that even professional fund managers have a rather lacklustre record of timing market movements. However, the rewards of being correct are so substantial that those who have the inclination—and can take the heat—should go ahead.

No matter whether your approach is active or passive, you need to develop a target structure. Let's see now how you can construct a mutual fund portfolio that will protect you against uncertain and adverse economic change, and how you should subsequently modify it to keep in step with changing times.

Portfolio structures

The secret of successful long-term fund investment is to diversify appropriately, to build a portfolio that will immunize you against the shocks of rising interest rates, high inflation rates and volatile equity market moves. To this end, you need a portfolio balance that provides steady income and growth opportunities and, above all, one that will preserve your capital as measured in terms of its purchasing power.

People at different life stages have different requirements. The target portfolios outlined in Table 6 are designed for investors at four very different stages. For each of them, we have constructed two portfolios, an essentially conservative portfolio, one that will best suit most investors. However, we have also appended a more aggressive version which has higher proportions of equity funds and will hence fluctuate more in value. We recommend the aggressive stance only for investors who have a high risk tolerance.

The components of the portfolios as you'll see, include several of the types of funds whose characteristics were explored in Chapter 2.

Portfolio 1 is designed for a single woman, age 35. Her primary objective is growth and she is worried about the effects of inflation on her capital. Yet she desires some capital preservation as she wants to limit the yearly fluctuations in her investments. Given these needs, about 35 per cent of her portfolio should be in large, well-diversified, bellwether equity funds for long-term growth opportunities; 25 per cent should be in fixed-income funds, bonds and mortgages; while 25 per cent should be directed to money market funds. The latter, although typically providing lower current yields than long-term bond funds, better protects the portfolio against rising interest rates should inflation increase in the future. The remaining 15 per cent invested in gold or precious metal funds will protect her against severe inflation or economic turmoil. This structure will provide reasonable growth prospects in the equity component yet serve to protect capital in the fixed income component.

Portfolio 2 is designed for a young married couple starting a family. Their investment time horizon is very long and therefore they can ride out the ups and downs in the stock market. On the other hand, the expenses required to bring up a family are high and they may require part of their savings for this purpose. Their mix of investments should be fairly balanced between equity and fixed-income securities.

Portfolio 3 is designed for a married breadwinner, age 40–50 at the peak earning stage of his or her career. We will assume that many of the expenses in bringing up a family have already been incurred and that this investor has surplus employment income available for savings. Investment time horizon is long-term in that retirement is still 15–25 years into the future. The investment portfolio should be diversified with a bias towards growth.

Portfolio 4 is aimed at a married couple, age 55 plus, who

TABLE 6 Asset Mix: Sample Portfolios

Fund type	*Portfolio 1 Single Woman Age 35 %*	*Portfolio 2 Married Couple Age 25–35 %*	*Portfolio 3 Married Breadwinner Age 35–50 %*	*Portfolio 4 Married Couple Approaching Retirement Age 55 + %*
Conservative version				
Canadian Equity	25	20	30	—
International Equity	10	10	10	10
Bond & Mortgage	25	30	20	35
Balanced	—	—	10	20
Gold & Precious Metals	15	10	10	—
Money Market	25	30	20	35
Total	100	100	100	100
Aggressive Version				
Canadian Equity	30	25	35	10
International Equity	20	15	15	10
Bond & Mortgage	15	30	10	30
Balanced	—	—	10	20
Gold & Precious Metals	15	10	10	—
Money Market	20	20	20	30
Total	100	100	100	100

are approaching retirement and who want above all to preserve their capital. The majority of their assets should be invested in fixed-income securities. The bond and mortgage funds will provide a consistent level of income throughout their retirement years while money market funds will insulate the portfolio against resurgent inflation. (Remember that high inflation brings high interest rates which will benefit money market funds.) Only smaller amounts should be invested in equity or balanced funds.

As we have seen, the best fund investment strategy for most people involves planning for the long term — buying funds and holding them in the expectation of preserving and increasing your purchasing power. But even those adopting the passive approach should revise their portfolios from time to time to reflect changing conditions. There are, essentially, three issues here.

First, you should continually monitor the individual mutual funds in your portfolio, watching for changes in risk categories, consistency of performance, management changes and so on. (You'll learn about the analytic tools you'll need for monitoring change in Chapter 7.) If you note a radical adverse change in a fund's performance or management, you may want to replace it with another.

Secondly, you should change the composition of your portfolio as your financial situation and prospects change, for example as your children approach college age or as retirement nears. As you age your portfolio should become less risky—to the point where you hold virtually no equities by the time you turn 55. The sample portfolios in Table 6 will serve as guidelines.

Finally, you should revise your portfolio to reflect changing external economic conditions. Here, in a sense, you will be operating your portfolio as if you were managing a balanced fund. Your overall strategy is to periodically adjust the percentage weights of your portfolio back to the target structure.

For example, if a strong stock market rally substantially increases the value of the equity component, you should switch from equity into fixed-income funds until the equity component is back to the targeted percentage. Similarly, if the equity portion falls well below the target percentage, possibly during a bear market, you sell fixed-income units to buy additional equity funds. Or, if there has been a sharp rise in gold prices, you'll be selling precious metal funds until that component is back to the target percentage.

The result of this balancing strategy is that you will normally be selling on market rallies and buying on dips, capturing economic cycles—a very professional and unemotional approach to investing. If you employ this strategy prudently, you will probably make modest revisions only every four or five years or so, the normal duration of a market cycle.

If you use this strategy, you should have a goodly portion of your portfolio in funds that belong to "families" such as the Mackenzie Financial Corporation's Industrial Group of funds, to make switching easier and less costly. If you choose a family that charges no loads, such as Royal Trust's, you may pay no transfer fee at all. No-load funds that do impose a transfer fee usually charge only $15 to $25. Some funds offer a limited number of switches, others impose no limits.

Active revision strategies

If you are an active investor, you'll attempt to time your investments to beat the market. You will hold equity funds during bull markets, and Treasury bills, bonds and cash during bears. Only those willing to devote substantial effort and time and have the expertise should attempt this.

Using this approach, of course, you'll time your revisions to conform with your projections of market cycles. If you conclude that the economy is overheated and that a slowdown is imminent, you'll sell your equity and bond holdings and move into money market funds. The second part of Table 7 shows how you should structure your portfolio in a bear market. The equity component is cut to the bone (a small percentage is retained in common share and balanced funds just in case you are wrong!), while most of your assets move to money market funds. As the recession deepens, you slowly move your money back into the bond and stock markets, first into bond funds, then into equities. At the start of the next bull market your portfolio will look like that in the first part of Table 7, with a substantial allocation to equity

TABLE 7 Bull and Bear Market Mutual Fund Portfolios

Fund type	*Portfolio 1 Single Woman Age 35 %*	*Portfolio 2 Married Couple Age 25–35 %*	*Portfolio 3 Married Breadwinner Age 35–50 %*	*Portfolio 4 Married Couple Age 55 + %*
Beginning of Bull market				
Canadian equity	40	30	40	20
International equity	25	20	20	15
Bond and mortgage	10	20	10	10
Balanced	—	—	10	20
Gold or precious metals	10	10	10	5
Money market	15	20	10	30
Total	100	100	100	100
Beginning of Bear market				
Canadian equity	5	5	5	5
International equity	5	5	5	—
Bond and mortgage	10	10	10	10
Balanced	10	10	10	10
Gold or precious metals	10	10	10	10
Money market	60	60	60	65
Total	100	100	100	100

funds and only a modest amount in fixed-income investments. As the bull market ages, however, you slowly readjust your weightings back to the targets as shown in Table 6.

Remember the caveat, however; you had better be extremely good at timing. There are substantial costs—and not just monetary ones—involved in switching; you will be investing considerable time and energy in your revision program. And the costs of being wrong can be enormous, particularly if you mistime the start of the next bear (or bull) market and hence mistime your switch out of (or into) equities. Suppose for example, that you had decided to get out of your equity funds on October 19, 1987 and had been lucky (?) enough to get through to your broker or to the fund itself. As it turned out you would have sold at the precise bottom of the crash!

Frankly, active investing is very difficult to do right over the long term.

CHAPTER 6

How to Evaluate the Performance of a Mutual Fund

by Eric Kirzner

You have decided to invest in mutual funds, and a study of the previous chapters in this book has already shown you which category or categories of fund will best meet your needs. But how do you now select the specific funds you'll buy into? The decision isn't easy. The universe of Canadian mutual funds is large and growing larger. And a wealth of information is available. It's the old, good news/bad news syndrome. The good news is that the financial press publishes lots of data. The bad news is that you have to come up with some systematic way of dealing with this seemingly overwhelming supply of information.

For instance, consider the following information that you could have gathered from data in the October 19, 1987 edition (don't forget that date, we'll get back to it later!) of *The Financial Post's* mutual fund performance survey:

Over the 10-year period from October 1, 1977 to September 30, 1987, the Industrial Growth Fund, a Canadian RRSP-eligible equity mutual fund, earned an annual compounded rate of return for its holders of 19.6 per cent (before fees). This means that a $10,000 investment made on October 1, 1977 would have grown to $59,884 by September 30, 1987, if all dividend and capital gain distributions had been reinvested in the fund's units. Over the same period, Canadian Security Growth Fund, an equity fund with similar characteristics, earned 21.7 per cent, so $10,000 would have grown to $71,270. A portfolio of Canadian stocks, as measured by the Toronto Stock Exchange 300 Composite total return index, showed a 19.2 per cent return over the period, meaning $10,000 would have grown to $57,911, while an investment in three-month Canadian Treasury bills yielded 10.9 per cent, meaning $10,000 would have grown to $28,139.

What does all of this mean? Well, some conclusions can quickly be drawn.

First, both mutual funds outperformed an investment in Treasury bills by a wide margin. Second, both funds outperformed a randomly selected portfolio of Canadian equities as measured by that TSE index. Finally, Canadian Security Growth Fund appeared in retrospect to have been the better bet for an investor who actually held the shares for those 10 years, as it yielded a higher return than Industrial Growth.

This is useful information, but the analysis is incomplete. Was Canadian Security Growth a better buy than Industrial Growth in September 1987? Did its performance justify the risk inherent in the fund's portfolio over that period? Were there, in fact, other mutual funds in the RRSP-eligible equity classification that dominated both? A deeper and more critical analysis would have been necessary before you could have made an informed decision as to which, if either, fund to invest in. This is what performance evaluation is all about.

In this chapter, you will learn about sources of information for the past performance of mutual funds and the methods you should use to measure relative historic mutual fund performance. You will learn about the most important criteria to use when evaluating historic data, both before you buy and in monitoring the performance of funds you own.

These evaluation methods encompass two important principles. First, performance should be measured either against other funds with similar objectives, or against appropriate benchmark indexes or portfolios. Second, these comparisons should reflect both risk and return.

Here's an illustration. Suppose you are examining the past

performance of XYZ, a balanced mutual fund. The company has enjoyed a 10-year annual compounded rate of return of 14 per cent. However, balanced mutual funds have on average realized a return of 12.5 per cent over the same period. Your initial reaction is to conclude that XYZ outperformed the average balanced fund. However, XYZ may have had a riskier portfolio than the average, and its net asset value may have fluctuated more than that of other balanced funds. This means that unitholders who had to sell XYZ at disadvantageous times probably ended up receiving a relatively low price. Furthermore, XYZ may very well be more vulnerable to market downturns than the average balanced fund.

Sources of information for performance evaluation

Your two major sources of information about mutual funds are the prospectuses of the funds and the published performance data found in the various newspapers and periodicals.

You have already learned in Chapter 4 how to find your way around a mutual fund's prospectus and other financial documents, and what you can deduce from the information in them. Now you need the published performance data to enable you to draw comparisons.

In the financial press, regular surveys of the 400 or so Canadian mutual funds give you the following data, all essential in order to make comparisons:

- annual compound rate of return over various time periods;
- variability class (the higher the variability, the wider the swings in net asset values and returns);
- initial launch date;
- RRSP eligibility;
- total assets;
- net asset value per share;
- maximum load fees;
- length of tenure of the fund manager.

You'll find this information and most of the calculations required, in several Canadian publications. *The Financial Post* publishes a monthly mutual fund's performance survey (annual subscription to *The Financial Post* is $39.95). The Financial Post Information Service puts out a quarterly *Survey of Funds* (annual subscription, $104). The *Financial Times of Canada* publishes a monthly funds survey (annual subscription to the newspaper is $30.00). Vancouver-based Comstat Pension Measurement Centre, a division of B.G. Hitchens Capital Management, produces a quarterly survey (annual subscription, $75).

Data on U.S. mutual funds can be found in the following U.S. publications: *Forbes*, *Johnson Charts*, the *Lipper Report*, *Standard & Poor's Mutual Fund Summary*, the *United Mutual Fund Selector*, *Barron's Weekly* and *Money Guide Mutual Funds*. International sources include the *Financial Times of London* (United Kingdom) and *Euromoney* (international). All publish periodic and annual tallies of mutual fund performance.

Sample survey pages from two of the most thorough mutual fund reporting publications, *The Financial Times of Canada* and *The Financial Post*, are shown below in figures 1 and 2.

FIGURE 1 Sample page from The Financial Times of Canada Mutual Funds Survey, December 21, 1987.

Mutual Fund	Net asset value $	Dividends $	% chg 1 mo.	% chg 3 mo.	% chg 1 yr.	Avg. annual compound rates of return 3 yr	5 yr	10yr	Total assets $ mil	% fgn	Max. sales fee	Codes	Times variability ranking	
Corporate Investors Ltd.	10.80		-0.4	-16.8	-1.3	7.9	11.8	12.2	12	4	9.00		17	3.27
Corporate Investors Stock Fund	6.68		-7.6	-34.4	-21.7	9.9	13.2	15.5	38	2	9.00		85	5.21
Counsel Trust Real Estate Fd	15.77		1.6	4.7	18.0	....	....	....	56			NL	N/A	....
Crown Commitment Fund	14.25		0.1	-23.4	-7.4	....	....	....	4			P	N/A	....
Cundill Security Fund	13.76		-1.9	-15.6	3.6	14.0	16.4	....	14	4	8.75		23	3.47
DK All Seasons Fund	2.96		-3.9	-27.6	-21.2	2.7	1.2	8.5	1				88	5.55
DK Enterprise Fund	13.90		-0.4	-25.2	4.2	12.7	8.8	14.5	5	2			91	5.70
Dynamic Fund of Canada Ltd.	13.11		-0.4	-17.4	4.6	14.1	13.1	16.8	170	10	9.00		26	3.91
Dynamic Managed Portfolio	6.34		1.1	-9.4	7.8	....	....	....	69	10	9.00		N/A	....
Dynamic Precious Metals Fund	1.43		6.7	-8.9	38.8	21.4	....	....	36	6	9.00		96	6.58
Ethical Growth Fund	5.32		3.6	-5.7	5.1	....	....	....	17		5.00		N/A	....
Everest Special Equity Fund	9.96	0.006	-3.0	-27.6	....	....	....	....	6		5.00		N/A	....
F.M.O.Q. Fonds de Placement	11.35	0.035	-3.4	-17.2	2.6	10.2	....	....	2	25			20	3.39
F.M.O.Q. Omnibus	22.29		-1.4	-10.2	3.9	12.5	12.5	....	36	7			7	2.24
Fds Reer St-Laurent-Actions	8.88		-5.6	-24.6	-15.8	....	....	....	!			NLP	N/A	....
Fds Reer St-Laurent-Diversif	10.54		-1.6	-1.6	0.4	....	....	....	2			NLP	N/A	....
Ficadre Actions	11.37	0.038	-3.2	-25.6	-5.4	....	....	....	2			P	N/A	....
Ficadre Equilibre	10.34	0.039	-1.7	-14.2	0.7	....	....	....	3	1		P	N/A	....
Fiduciaires Fonds Actions	8.98		-2.7	-22.2	-11.3	....	....	....	7	8		NLP	N/A	....
Fiducie Pret Revenu Retraite	18.90		-2.2	-11.2	-1.2	8.9	10.3	11.0	35	7			6	2.20
Fiducie Pret Revenue Canadien	8.43		-2.2	-28.8	-8.6	2.5	6.5	9.2	16	2			73	4.84
First City Growth Fund	4.49		3.6	-22.4	....	....	....	....	11	8	8.50		N/A	....
First City Realfund	5.84			3.7	13.7	13.0	....	....	28		8.00		1	1.61
Fiscon Investment Fund-Balance	9.45		0.0	-8.0	5.6	11.7	13.3	14.3	9	3	9.00		5	2.06

* *Reprinted permission by The Financial Times of Canada.*

FIGURE 2 Sample page from The Financial Post's Mutual Funds Performance Survey, December 21, 1987.

MUTUAL FUNDS PERFORMANCE SURVEY

Fund name	RRSP & RRIF eligible	Launch date	Fund manager (Years)	Total net assets $ millions Nov.30, 1987	Net asset value per share	Average annual compound rate of return ‡ 10 yr. %	5 yr. %	3 yr. %	Simple rates of return 1 yr. %	6 mo. %	Variability 5 yr.	1 yr.	Reward/risk ratio 5 yr.	1 yr.	Expense ratio %	Maximum sales redempt. charge %
CANADIAN EQUITY FUNDS																
A I C Advantage	R	12/85	Ken Rae (Incep)	10.7	8.77	n.a.	n.a.	n.a.	−12.4	−23.1	n.a.	avg	n.a.	−0.11	1.90	9.0
All-Cdn Compound	R	10/54	Philip Spicer	14.6 (a)	14.75	+14.7	+11.5	+10.3	+1.2	−12.6	avg	avg	+0.24	+0.01	n.a.	(e)
All-Cdn Dividend	R	10/54	Philip Spicer	16.4	11.52	+14.8	+11.9	+10.6	+1.2	−12.6	avg	avg	+0.25	+0.01	2.00	9.0
Allied Canadian	R	12/85	Robin McIsaac (2 yrs)	3.1	4.11	n.a.	n.a.	n.a.	−20.8	−33.7	n.a.	avg	n.a.	−0.18	2.00	nil
AMD Canadian Blue Chip	R	11/85	Midland Doherty (Incep)	8.6	9.25	n.a.	n.a.	n.a.	−10.2	−22.1	n.a.	avg	n.a.	−0.11	2.27	9.0
Associate Investors	R	04/50	G.L. Frazer (Incep)	7.0	6.20	+13.6	+12.9	+9.3	−3.3	−14.6	avg −	avg −	+0.29	−0.05	1.78	1.0
Bullock Growth	R	12/70	Multiple	8.3	2.12	+10.5	+4.9	+5.9	−5.7	−21.2	avg	avg	+0.08	−0.05	2.38	9.0
CGF 4000	R	09/71	Bill Moore (1 yr)	4.2	5.43	+13.5	+11.1	+11.4	−9.2	−21.2	avg	avg	+0.19	−0.09	1.71	9.0
CGF Venture		01/73	David McLeish (1 yr)	0.3	2.96	+1.1	−7.8	−13.7	−17.3	−26.6	avg +	avg +	−0.09	−0.13	2.00	9.0
CMA Investment	R	03/66	MD Management Ltd.	708.7	24.55	+16.8	+16.1	+14.8	+3.8	−12.6	avg −	avg	+0.39	+0.05	0.75	(q)
Cambridge Growth	R	08/66	Sagit Management Ltd.	1.0	7.12	+16.5	+20.8	+23.5	+6.7	−12.2	avg	avg	+0.42	+0.08	2.00	8.75
Cambridge Resource	R	07/68	Sagit Management Ltd.	0.6	2.75	+9.8	+9.9	+9.4	−0.4	−19.1	avg	avg	+0.17	−0.00	2.00	8.75
Canada Cumulative	R	08/72	Peter Spark (1 yr)	123.2	13.58	+13.7	+9.9	+5.8	−8.4	−19.5	avg	avg	+0.19	−0.10	1.73	9.0
Canada Trust Equity	R	10/59	C.T. Invest. Coun.(Incep)	33.1	49.55	+15.6	+12.7	+11.5	+2.2	−15.2	avg	avg	+0.20	+0.02	1.26	nil
Canada Trust RSP Equity	R	10/57	C.T. Invest Coun.(Incep)	311.9	94.49	+14.1	+11.0	+8.5	−3.4	−19.5	avg	avg	+0.18	−0.03	0.86	nil
Cdn Anaesthetists	R	11/57	Sceptre Invest. Counsel	51.1	9.03	+19.1	+15.3	+13.0	+1.9	−13.6	avg	avg	+0.29	+0.02	0.79	nil
Canadian Gas & Energy	R	03/60	W. R. Farquharson	60.1	7.85	+10.6	+4.3	+6.6	+21.9	−18.9	avg +	avg +	+0.05	+0.17	2.10	9.0
Canadian Investment	R	12/32	Multiple	89.0	6.38	+12.4	+9.9	+6.7	−3.7	−17.1	avg	avg	+0.18	−0.04	1.45	9.0
Canadian Protected	R	12/84	Jean-Pierre Fruchet	5.9	13.23	n.a.	n.a.	n.a.	+15.2	+6.3	n.a.	avg −	n.a.	+1.01	2.00	nil
Cdn Security Growth	R	06/63	W. R. Farquharson	535.1	8.15	+18.9	+16.9	+11.8	−7.1	−18.5	avg	avg	+0.33	−0.09	1.56	9.0
Capital Growth	R	10/37	J.C. Stodgell	2.8	7.10	+14.2	+8.6	+7.1	−0.8	−16.9	avg	avg	+0.15	−0.00	0.91	9.0
CDA Common Stock	R	05/58	Impco Invest. Mgmt(4 yrs)	30.6	123.67	+16.1	+16.0	+15.8	+2.1	−13.8	avg	avg	+0.30	+0.02	n.a.	nil
Central Trust RSP Equity	R	12/68	Central Cap. Mgmt.	13.5	48.06	+16.8	+11.7	+9.6	−2.1	−16.3	avg	avg	+0.21	−0.02	1.00	nil
Co-op Trust Growth	R	09/68	Co-op. Invest. Coun.	5.5	11.97	+12.3	+10.6	+10.2	−6.5	−19.4	avg	avg	+0.18	−0.06	1.35	nil
Confed Dolphin	R	10/72	Confed Invest. Mgmt. Ltd.	5.0	7.81	+16.6	+15.0	+11.4	−6.9	−18.9	avg	avg	+0.30	−0.08	1.50	5.5
Corporate Investors	R	07/31	J.L. Boeckh	11.5	10.80	+12.8	+11.8	+7.9	−1.3	−13.8	avg −	avg −	+0.30	−0.02	1.27	9.0
Corporate Inv Stock	R	04/68	W. R. Farquharson	38.3	6.68	+16.3	+13.2	+10.0	−21.7	−34.4	avg	avg	+0.21	−0.19	1.85	9.0
Cundill Security	R	79	Peter Cundill (12 yrs)	14.2	13.76	n.a.	+16.9	+14.0	+3.6	−9.8	avg −	avg −	+0.39	+0.06	1.73	8.75
Dixon Krogseth Enterprise	R	07/70	Dixon Krogseth Ltd.	4.7	13.90	+15.7	+8.8	+12.7	+4.2	−22.3	avg	avg	+0.12	+0.03	1.86	1.0
Domequity Growth	R	12/67	R.B. Love (5 yrs)	3.8	8.06	+0.8	−5.1	−8.4	−10.7	−35.8	avg +	avg +	−0.06	−0.08	2.00	0.5
Dynamic Canada	R	07/57	Beutel Goodman (Incep)	170.1	13.11	+17.0	+12.9	+14.2	+4.6	−11.8	avg	avg	+0.26	+0.06	2.00	9.0

* *Reprinted with permission from The Financial Fost.*

What is in the tables?

The Canadian performance-ranking publications normally group the funds surveyed by type, making it easier for investors to conduct their comparative analyses. However, their classifications are far broader than those you have become accustomed to in your reading of this book. For instance, within the group "Equity funds RSP eligible," you are likely to find many types of funds, including real estate, balanced and index, so you will still have to do a little hunting.

How do these Canadian sources stack up one against another in terms of the amount of information they give? Tables 1 to 5 provide a convenient summary of the data found in each one.

As you will see, the services show some consistency in their data, but none of them provide everything. It is likely that either *The Financial Post* or *Financial Times* surveys will provide enough for your needs; however, it may be necessary to go to two or more services if some special analytic information is required.

While most of the items shown in Tables 1 to 5 are self-explanatory, a few require elaboration as follows:

The compound rate of return measures the annual total return to investors. It includes capital appreciation/depreciation (increase/decrease in the fund's net asset value), plus interest, dividend and capital gain distributions, which are assumed to be reinvested in the month distributed. These total returns are averaged over a number of years, typically 10, five and three.

The simple rate of return measures the total return to investors over the period, typically one year, three months and year-to-date, and includes the capital appreciation (increase in the fund's net asset value), plus interest, dividend and capital gain distributions, which are assumed to be reinvested in the month distributed.

Variability measures the degree to which a fund's return fluctuates from month to month and is reported by the standard deviation, a well-known statistical measure. Variability equates with risk. Everything else being equal, you should prefer a fund with a low variance over a fund with a higher one.

TABLE 1 Canadian Performance-Ranking Publications—Comparative Data

Publication	*RRSP/RRIF Eligibility*	*Launch Date*	*Name of Fund Manager and Years Operating Fund*	*Total Assets*	*Net Asset Value Per Share*	*Dividends in Latest Month*
Financial Post Funds Survey (monthly)	Yes	Yes	Yes	Yes	Yes	No
Financial Post Survey of Funds (quarterly)	Yes	No	Yes	Yes	No	No
Comstat RRSP and Mutual Fund Survey (quarterly)	Yes	No	No	Yes	Yes	Yes
Financial Times of Canada Funds Survey (monthly)	Yes	No	No	Yes	No	No

TABLE 2 *Canadian Performance-Ranking Publications—Comparative Data* (continued)

	Compounded Rates of Return			
Publication	*10-Year*	*5-Year*	*3-Year*	*All Years Starting 10 Years Ago*
Financial Post Funds Survey (monthly)	Yes	Yes	Yes	No
Financial Post Survey of Funds (quarterly)	Yes, plus ranking	Yes, plus ranking	Yes, plus ranking	Yes
Comstat RRSP and Mutual Fund Survey (quarterly)	Yes, plus ranking	Yes, plus ranking	Yes, plus ranking	Yes, plus ranking
Financial Times of Canada Funds Survey (monthly)	Yes	Yes	Yes	No

TABLE 3 Canadian Performance-Ranking Publications—Comparative Data *(continued)*

		Simple Rates of Return				
Publication	*Year Over 10 Years*	*1-Year*	*6-Months*	*3-Months*	*1-Month*	*Year To Date*
Financial Post Funds Survey (monthly)	No	Yes	Yes	No	No	No
Financial Post Survey of Funds (quarterly)	Yes	Yes, plus ranking	No	Yes	No	Yes
Comstat RRSP and Mutual Fund Survey (quarterly)	No	Yes, plus ranking	No	Yes, plus ranking	No	Yes, plus ranking
Financial Times of Canada Funds Survey (monthly)	No	Yes	No	Yes	Yes	No

TABLE 4 Canadian Performance-Ranking Publications—Comparative Data (continued)

	Variability		Reward/Risk Ratio		Expense Ratio
Publication	*5-Year*	*1-Year*	*5-Year*	*1-Year*	
Financial Post Funds Survey (monthly)	Yes, as avg +, avg, and avg −	Yes, as avg +, avg, and avg −	Yes, as return/ standard deviation	Yes, as return/ standard deviation	Yes, as per cent of assets
Financial Post Survey of Funds (quarterly)	Yes, standard deviation	Yes, standard deviation	Yes, as return/ standard deviation	Yes, as return/ standard deviation	No
Comstat RRSP and Mutual Fund Survey (quarterly)	No	No	No	No	No
Financial Times of Canada Funds Survey (monthly)	No	Yes, standard deviation, plus percentile ranking	No	No	No

TABLE 5 *Canadian Performance-Ranking Publications—Comparative Data* *(continued)*

Publication	*Maximum Load Charge*	*Market Indicators*	*Category Group Averages*
Financial Post Funds Survey (monthly)	Yes	Yes	Yes
Financial Post Survey of Funds (quarterly)	No	Yes	Yes
Comstat RRSP and Mutual Fund Survey (quarterly)	No	Yes	Yes
Financial Times of Canada Funds Survey (monthly)	Yes	Yes	Yes

The reward/risk ratio is the total return divided by the standard deviation. This is a combined performance ratio, incorporating both risk and return. The reward/risk ratio specifically provides the return (reward) per unit of risk (standard deviation).

A framework for evaluating performance

Your objective here is to evaluate a fund's past performance, comparing it to the performance of funds within the same category. Here are the factors that the professionals consider when making their evaluations:

Return

The evaluator's first consideration is returns. The appropriate measure of return is the annual compounded rate of return, calculated as described above. You might also want to calculate what your returns would have been on an after-tax basis.

Risk

A common question novice investors ask is, ''Why worry about the risk of a fund?'' In short, if a fund realized a return of 20 per cent per year against an overall average of 15 per cent for all funds in the same category, then why be concerned? The fund, surely, has done well. That's a valid point. However, there are important reasons for identifying a fund's risk or variability.

Here, the primary purpose is to identify fund managers (or teams of managers) who exhibit above-average performance, *using skilful analytic techniques*. A fund manager who achieves a high rate of return over a specific period may have done so through sheer luck, or by holding an extremely risky portfolio. That same manager may perform poorly in the future, independent of market performance, or may suffer large losses when the market is weak. On the other hand, a fund manager who has earned above-average returns consistently, with only modest or average variability has indeed earned those returns through skill. There is, of course, no absolute guarantee of similar performance in the future, but there is at least past evidence of superior management.

Additionally, a mutual fund that is subject to wide swings in value poses potential problems at exit time. You may be forced to cash in your units just when their net asset value is plunging.

What you are looking for, then, is consistency—a fund that performs reasonably well during both favorable and unfavorable times. There is a curious and important arithmetic associated with rates of returns. If your mutual fund rises in value by 50 per cent and then falls in value by 50 per cent, how have you done? Broken even? Not on your life! You have lost 25 per cent! Look at the arithmetic: if you invest $1,000, you end up with $1,000 × 1.50 × .5 = $750. The same result holds if you first lose 50 per cent and then gain 50 per cent: $1,000 × .50 × 1.50 = $750. Funds with wide swings are clearly dangerous. Instead, look for funds that perform consistently and satisfactorily in both up and down markets.

Two risk measures can be used to evaluate fund performance: the standard deviation and beta.

The standard deviation, generally the more appropriate method for fund investors, measures the degree of total variability in the fund's rate of return and hence measures the risk inherent in the fund. The higher the standard deviation, the greater the variability of returns. This standard deviation should then be compared with that of an appropriate benchmark index. If, like most investors, you want to minimize risk and earn consistent returns, you will avoid funds with very high standard deviations on both an absolute and a comparative basis, everything else being equal.

The Financial Post provides a broad measure of standard deviation by classifying funds as either average, above average (avg +) or below average (avg −), when compared to all the funds in the same objective category. The *Financial Times* uses a numeric measure showing how much a fund's return is likely to deviate from its monthly average (hence a fund with a standard deviation of 8.00 is twice as volatile as a fund whose deviation is measured at 4.00). Additionally, a percentile ranking system shows how each fund rates against all others in the same group; for instance, a fund with a ranking of 10 is less volatile than 90 per cent of all the funds in the grouping, and more volatile than only 9 per cent.

The beta measure of risk is calculated by relating the return on a fund to that of an appropriate market index. (An equity fund would be compared to the Toronto Stock Exchange 300 Composite total return index). In non-technical terms, this means that it is an indicator of how a fund's value has fluctuated relative to past changes in an appropriate benchmark. The higher the fund's beta, the greater the degree of fluctuation for a given change in the overall market. A high beta equity fund therefore would be expected to realize high rates of returns when the stock market was strong, but relatively large losses when the market was weak. A low beta fund would be expected to have relatively lower rates of returns when the market was strong, but suffer smaller losses when the market was weak.

Consistency

Studies show that one year's high-performing funds are sometimes the big losers the next year. Some funds outperform the averages in strong markets, but underperform in weak ones. And often mutual funds on average do not outperform a randomly selected portfolio of securities. A key criterion in selecting a good fund is *consistency* of performance; how well the fund performs in bad markets as well as good. The firm's standard deviation, beta, and reward-to-risk measures are therefore all important.

As an example of consistency, consider the First Canadian Mortgage Fund. It achieved an average annual compounded return of 11.4 per cent between July 1, 1977 and June 30, 1987. It achieved positive returns in all of those 10 years and showed reasonably consistent performance throughout. Its only weak year was 1980, when it earned 3.2 per cent, but that was a year in which the average return for all Canadian fixed-income funds was 0.4 per cent.

Stability of management

Next, you should determine the length of tenure of the fund's manager, and whether the one who managed the fund's portfolio when it produced big gains is still at the helm. ''Hot'' managers are sometimes lured into a better-paying competitor's camp, and a mutual fund with a spectacular track record may not be a good bet for the future if there is a change in the management team. Often, the portfolio is managed by an advisory firm with a defined strategy. That can be a plus; it provides a degree of consistency when there's a turnover of individual managers.

The Financial Post's monthly funds survey shows fund managers and the number of years they have been in charge in most cases. (Some funds are run by a team, while others refuse to disclose the manager's identity.)

Time Frames

Wherever possible, you should select funds on the basis of annual performance over a long period such as five or 10 years, rather than on the basis of a year's record or even less. John Templeton, one of the world's most successful fund managers, suggests an examination of performance over two or more market cycles (each cycle is usually four-plus years) to see how the fund did in both bull and bear markets. For this purpose, check the records of funds that interest you over 1979–1981 and 1982–October 1987.

Combined performance measures

Return and risk measures can be combined to create a single measure of fund performance. One such indicator is the reward/risk ratio, calculated by dividing the fund's standard deviation into its return. Or the excess return (return above the risk-free rate) is divided by the standard deviation of the excess return. (This is known as the Sharpe measure.) Thus a reward/risk ratio measures the past return per unit of risk undertaken. Comparisons of mutual funds and between the funds and a benchmark index are a measure of past reward to variability.

Another useful measure is the reward per systematic-risk measure or the excess return divided by the beta of the portfolio. (This is known as the Treynor measure). Systematic risk, as you'll remember from Chapter 3, is the risk associated with the marketplace itself rather than the individual investment. Here's an illustration:

Two mutual funds, AAA and ZZZ, have rates of returns of

16 and 21 per cent respectively. Fund AAA's standard deviation is 6 per cent while ZZZ's is 26 per cent. The 91-day Treasury bill rate was 9 per cent over the period, while an appropriate benchmark index yielded 13 per cent.

The first thing that we note is that both funds yielded more than the risk-free rate of interest as measured by 91-day Treasury bills. They also outperformed the benchmark index. Fund AAA provided an excess return of 16 − 13 = 3 per cent, while ZZZ returned 21 − 13 = 8 per cent. However, AAA's reward/risk ratio translates into 3 ÷ 6 = 0.50, while ZZZ's is 8 ÷ 26 = 0.31. So in terms of return per unit of risk, AAA actually outperformed ZZZ. Fund ZZZ appears to hold a risky portfolio; it earned a higher rate of return than AAA, but it also has a higher likelihood of suffering a substantial loss.

Putting it all together: a filter approach

Fund analysis, we can now see, involves several separate steps. First, you should examine the 10-year record probably representing two, sometimes three, market cycles. (A good starting point is to look at funds which have been among the top 10 performers over that period.) Then you look to see how it has performed relative to a benchmark index and to the other funds in the same category, in both strong and weak markets. Next you check to see if the manager who achieved the results is still in place. Your objective is to find a fund with a consistent track record, a strong history, and preferably the same manager. Some of the funds that have been launched recently look very interesting but keep in mind that there isn't a long-term record to examine. Finally, you'll use the various performance measures to reduce a long selection list to a short one, and ultimately to the fund or funds you'll buy.

A specific approach

Here's a step-by-step filter approach to mutual fund selection. Why filter? Because we start with the whole universe of mutual funds, then methodically filter out unsuitable candidates.

STEP 1 Identify the category or categories of funds that will best meet your goals. You have probably already done this with the help of Chapters 1, 2 and 5. The Canadian fund surveys group funds into categories fairly consistently, although there are some minor variations, and you'll be very familiar with most categories by now. (If you need to refresh your memory, turn back to Chapter 2.) They are:

- equity or growth funds;
- balanced funds;
- dividend income funds;
- specialty funds;
- fixed-income funds;
- money market funds;
- real estate funds;
- index funds;
- single-country funds (which invest all of their assets in one specific country);
- global and international.

You will not yet be familiar with the terminology of that last category. Mutual funds specializing in overseas investment are classified by the investment community as either international or global. There is an important distinction. International funds are those that invest only into markets outside the domestic country. They may even restrict their activities to a specific region or continent. By contrast, global funds have no geographic bounds; they invest anywhere management believes bargains can be found—including their own domestic markets. Global funds thus offer greater diversification than international funds because of this lack of restriction on investment activities. (However, an investor could buy into both a diversified Canadian fund and an international fund to replicate a global portfolio.)

STEP 2 Now eliminate all funds whose average annual compound rates of return over the past 10 years are below the average for all funds in the category, as well as all those that had below-average reward/risk ratios. If the type of fund you have chosen is included with several other types in a publication's broad grouping, a comparison with that grouping's average may not be very meaningful; you will probably want to spend a little more time making comparisons among various funds of the type that interests you.

STEP 3 You probably now have a short list of five to 10 funds. You make your next selection by examining recent returns (is performance improving or deteriorating?); consistency of returns (are the year-over-year returns relatively stable?); performance in bull and bear markets (which funds seemed to hold up best in the weak markets, such as in 1980–82, or in October-December, 1987?).

At this stage you will also consider management objectives, to be found, as you learned in Chapter 4, in the fund's prospectuses, as well as details on the kinds of investments management is empowered to make. You'll check portfolio revisions by reading the quarterly, semi-annual and annual reports. And you'll check on management's length of tenure in the surveys.

You will also consider loads and other types of fees which, especially if you are not investing for the long term, may whittle down the overall return on your investment quite substantially. As you know already, the prime costs are the front-end load, payable at purchase and — less commonly — the rear-end load, payable on redemption. You'll learn more about these, and about several other lesser-known costs, in Chapter 8.

For the time being, just ignore the popular myth that load funds generally perform better than those without loads. Studies indicate that the performance of no-load funds does not differ significantly from load funds.

If your short list is still not short enough, there are two more criteria you can use, but neither, in our opinion, embodies much merit.

The first is a fund's operating expenses. They may be measured as total operating costs per $100 of assets. *The Financial Post*'s surveys measure them as a percentage of assets under management. This statistic generally is known as the management expense ratio. Although studies indicate that high expense-ratio funds tend to slightly underperform low expense-ratio funds, the relationship is not a strong one and is likely to be dominated by other factors. In short, a low expense-ratio does not necessarily imply above average performance.

The second is the size of the pool of assets under management. Here, there is a popular belief that small mutual funds outperform large ones. Research studies are mixed on the relationship between size of fund and performance, but in general they show that the returns of small funds are similar to those of large ones.

The past as an indicator of the future

When a scientist combines hydrogen, sulphur and oxygen in certain proportions under controlled laboratory conditions, the result is sulphuric acid. The rate at which a falling object falls always accelerates by 16 feet per second.

These are scientific facts, based on initial theory followed by empirical observation. This is a world of certainty. The financial world, however, is a world of uncertainty. True, over long periods of time (25 years or more), stocks have yielded higher returns than bonds, and bonds have outperformed Treasury bills, and this is likely to be the case in the future. Far less certain is what will happen in the near-term. For example, Treasury bills produced far higher returns than stocks in 1980–82.

Past performance data for mutual funds and benchmark indexes must therefore be interpreted with caution. There is no guarantee that the future will reflect the past. But a careful analysis of past data does provide clues to the future. We can discover which funds and which fund managers did indeed reward their investors with returns appropriate for the risk class, and hence justified their management fees.

An analysis in action: examining returns

To illustrate our thesis, we have examined the returns achieved by six representative equity mutual funds domiciled in Canada. The results are shown in Table 6 below. In each case, we show the annual compounded rate of return for 10 years (1977–87) and five years (1982–87), as well as the value today of a $5,000 investment made 10 and five years ago. For comparative purposes, the annual compounded rates of returns for the Toronto Stock Exchange 300 Composite total return index, and that for three-month Treasury bills are also shown.

TABLE 6 Pre-October 19, 1987
Rates of Returns on Selected Canadian Equity Mutual Funds, The TSE 300 Total Return Index, and 91-Day Treasury Bills

	Period ending September 30, 1987 Before commissions or load			
	Average Annual Rate of Return		*Value of $5,000 Investment*	
Mutual Fund	*10-Year (%)*	*5-Year (%)*	*10-Year*	*5-Year*
Canadian Security Growth	21.7	25.2	$35,635	$15,381
Dynamic Canada	19.1	19.5	$28,714	$12,185
Industrial Growth	19.6	25.0	$29,942	$15,259
Montreal Trust Equity	16.5	18.3	$23,027	$11,585
Royfund Equity	21.2	27.6	$34,198	$16,913
Univest Growth	14.8	14.6	$19,879	$ 9,883
TSE 300 Total Return Index	19.2	23.7	$28,956	$14,482
3-Month Treasury Bills	10.9	9.8	$14,070	$ 7,980

After commissions or load

	Average Annual Rate of Return		*Value of $5,000 Investment*	
Mutual Fund	*10-Year (%)*	*5-Year (%)*	*10-Year*	*5-Year*
Canadian Security Growth	20.6	22.9	$32,428	$13,997
Dynamic Canada	17.9	17.3	$25,911	$11,088
Industrial Growth	18.5	22.7	$27,247	$13,885
Montreal Trust Equity	16.5	18.3	$23,027	$11,585
Royfund Equity	21.2	27.6	$34,198	$16,913
Univest Growth	13.7	12.5	$18,090	$ 8,994
TSE 300 Total Return Index	18.8	22.9	$28,087	$14,047
3-Month Treasury Bills	10.9	9.8	$14,070	$ 7,980

TABLE 7 Post-October 19, 1987
Rates of Returns on Selected Canadian Equity Mutual Funds,
The TSE 300 Total Return Index, and 91-Day Treasury Bills

	Period ending October 30, 1987 Before commissions or load			
	Average Annual Rate of Return		*Value of $5,000 Investment*	
Mutual Fund	*10-Year (%)*	*5-Year (%)*	*10-Year*	*5-Year*
Canadian Security Growth	19.2	18.7	$28,956	$11,782
Dynamic Canada	17.1	13.6	$24,240	$ 9,459
Industrial Growth	17.0	17.3	$24,034	$11,104
Montreal Trust Equity	14.1	12.0	$18,699	$ 8,812
Royfund Equity	18.6	19.8	$27,531	$12,338
Univest Growth	13.1	10.6	$17,124	$ 8,275
TSE 300 Total Return Index	16.2	15.1	$22,440	$10,101
3-Month Treasury Bills	10.9	9.8	$14,070	$ 7,980

After commissions or load

Mutual Fund	*Average Annual Rate of Return*		*Value of $5,000 Investment*	
	10-Year (%)	*5-Year (%)*	*10-Year*	*5-Year*
Canadian Security Growth	18.1	16.5	$26,350	$10,722
Dynamic Canada	16.0	11.5	$22,059	$ 8,608
Industrial Growth	15.9	15.1	$21,871	$10,104
Montreal Trust Equity	14.1	12.0	$18,699	$ 8,812
Royfund Equity	18.6	19.8	$27,531	$12,338
Univest Growth	12.0	8.5	$15,583	$ 7,530
TSE 300 Total Return Index	15.8	14.4	$21,767	$ 9,798
3-Month Treasury Bills	10.9	9.8	$14,070	$ 7,980

These returns are shown both before and after brokerage commissions or fund loads. For the latter calculation, we've assumed that the maximum mutual-fund sales charge (9 per cent) was paid at purchase and that brokerage commissions were 3 per cent.

As you'll see, all the funds provided returns higher than those 30-day Treasury bills. If, for example, an investment of $5,000 (of which $4,550 went to the purchase of shares and $450 for commissions) had been made in the Canadian Security Growth Fund in 1977, and if all dividends had been reinvested immediately, the investor would have had $32,428 in September 1987, or an annual compounded rate of return of 20.6 per cent. That same amount invested in a representative portfolio of Canadian common shares, as approximated by the TSE 300 Index, with dividends reinvested, would have been worth only $28,087 or 18.8 per cent compounded.

Table 7 shows the situation just one month later—after the October 19th market crash. A comparison of the results provides some rich material. Although the funds were clearly hurt during the crash, the strong performers were still showing healthy 10-year returns compared to the TSE 300 and Treasury bills. However, the five-year returns showed more dramatic effects, illustrating the importance of long-term mutual fund investment strategies. Of course there is no guarantee that the past performance of these funds will be duplicated in the future.

Conclusion

The overall performance record of mutual funds is mixed. Earlier studies of relative performance indicated that, on average, they outperform the market. However, more recent studies are ambiguous. Close examination of the data does indicate that a few funds consistently outperform both the general market and the majority of other funds. These are the ones that you should identify. Your prime task, in short, is to find the truly professional and successful managers.

CHAPTER 7

How To Pick the Fund That's Best For You

by Keith A. Douglas

Investment counsellors and portfolio managers are educated and trained in the art of investment analysis and selection. They usually also have a good comprehension of economics and are able to interpret various economic developments into specific investment decisions. Many of them manage large investment portfolios for institutions: pension funds, charitable foundations, insurance companies, banks, trust companies and mutual funds.

In cases where investment counsellors act for individuals, they acquire and manage many securities specifically chosen to meet the client's unique objectives. They modify the portfolio on an ongoing basis to suit both changing economic conditions and the client's changing needs. Generally speaking, investment counsellors will not perform this function for individuals who have less than $250,000 to invest. In many cases the required minimum can be as high as $1 million.

And all those other people who wish to invest in securities but don't have sufficient assets to meet these minimums? They, of course, are the people for whom the mutual fund was conceived.

We've started with this preamble because we want you to view buying into a mutual fund in the same light as hiring a portfolio manager.

However, a fund's portfolio manager manages a portfolio of securities in keeping with the stated objectives of the fund. And, as we've already seen, those objectives may not be the same as your own so, unlike hiring a personal counsellor to custom-tailor a portfolio for you, *you* have the responsibility for selecting the correct funds to achieve your objectives.

Earlier in this book—notably in Chapters 1 and 5—you did some preliminary exercises and studied some sample portfolios to help you select the right fund or funds for you. In this chapter, we'll take a closer look at that matchmaking process and pull all the threads together.

Assessing your objectives

For all of the money we decide not to spend, but rather to save, we have some purpose in mind. It may be a major purchase, a child's college education, a vacation, an emergency fund or simply our own future welfare.

Whatever the purpose, you'll probably find it easy to answer two questions about the money saved for these purposes.

1. When will I need to use this money for the purpose for which I saved it?

2. Does it matter to me if the value of my invested money fluctuates in the meantime?

If your answer to the first question indicates that you'll need the money soon, you will probably answer ''Yes'' to the second question. Investments made for the short term are best placed in investments whose objectives are also short-term. You'll also likely want to maximize income from your investment.

In such a case, among mutual funds you'd probably choose a money market fund. Such funds, you'll recall, hold very short-term debt instruments and rarely fluctuate in value.

Buying into an aggressive equity fund in this situation would be folly; its value could be down when you needed your money.

But if your answer to the first question indicates a long period of time, then you might answer ''No'' to the second one. In this case, many kinds of funds are possible investments for you and it's simply a matter of refining your objective.

You may have other needs. Perhaps you'll decide that you require high current income, or that you're paying too much tax and hence need more tax-efficient income. It could be that you require long-term capital growth. Or maybe you'll decide you need a mix of investments.

Whatever the case, *you* must decide specifically what you want to accomplish by making an investment.

In Chapter 1, you saw how broad investment types might be expected to meet (or fail to meet) your personal goals. Let's now do a similar exercise, this time specifically examining mutual funds.

Objectives	*Appropriate Fund Type*
Long-term growth	Equity funds
Tax-efficient income/safety	Preferred income/dividend funds
Long-term/high income	Bond funds
Medium-term/high income	Mortgage funds
Tax-efficient income/	Real property funds
growth	Equity funds
Short-term/high income	Money market funds
Income/growth/safety	Balanced funds

The graphic illustration on the following page elaborates on how you might select a fund considering your objectives (Anticipated Return) and risk tolerance (Volatility Characteristics).

Risk

When it comes to investing, many people are preoccupied with risk, in other words, the safety of the money invested. This concern naturally increases as the time approaches when we'll need the money. We want to make sure it is all going to be there.

But there are other situations where people aren't concerned about risk. Buying a home is one example. The insurance available on real estate is only to protect the property against fire or other damage, not to protect its value in market downturns. Most people have a basic confidence that ownership of real estate will, in the long run, be beneficial, a perception that is reinforced

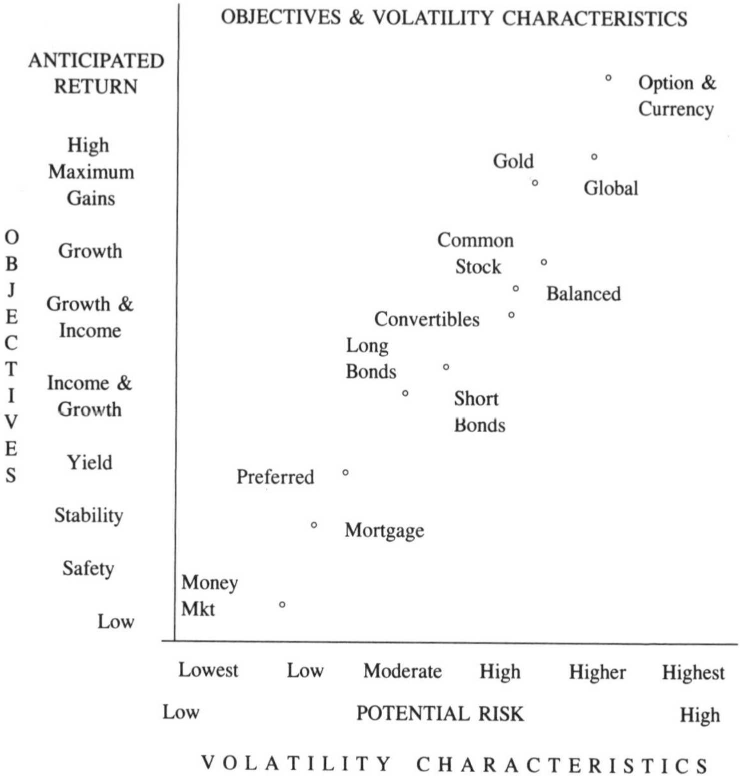

each time we see evidence that real estate values climb over long periods of time.

For all that, the value of real estate moves in cycles—up some years, down in others and static in yet others. The same is true of most kinds of investments that are not guaranteed: their value moves in cycles.

The same perception people hold about the value of a home —that it will go up in the long run—can be held about most equity investments. As with real estate, equity markets have proven time and time again that stocks increase in value over the long term.

As we saw in Chapter 6, the financial press regularly reports measurments of the degree of risk associated with mutual funds. Bear in mind, however, that these measurements don't furnish very broad comparisons for you. A reported high risk in a mutal fund doesn't necessarily indicate a huge risk — such as you'd incur, for instance, if you invested in a penny stock.

Philosophically one could say that risk is involved in just about any action. If, for example, you put your money into a five-year guaranteed investment certificate (GIC) returning 10 per cent, you risk a loss of opportunity if interest rates move to say, 13 per cent.

We have been taught to avoid risk. As children, we were admonished, "Don't go near the water!" or "Be careful of that knife!" But as we experience more of life, we learn that we can take calculated risks and still remain comfortable, largely because we have taken the trouble to understand the nature of the risk and hence feel that we are at least partially in control.

Investment risk should be regarded in precisely this way. With adequate knowledge and the ability to remain reasonably in control, investment risk can and should be managed.

Customizing your risk profile

We discussed earlier the need to identify the end purpose of the money you have available for investment. Next, we looked at types of funds that will best serve various purposes. Then we took a fresh look at the element of risk.

Now we need to put these three factors together to determine which kinds of funds are really most suitable for your personal investment program, a process commonly referred to as asset mixing.

In Chapter 5, you'll remember, we saw examples of conservative mutual fund portfolios structured to meet the needs of four investor profiles. The portfolios were then modified to show how the asset mix might be adjusted to respond to the needs of a more aggressive investor.

What you now need to assess is how closely those four investor profiles resemble *you*. Do you really represent that typical married couple in the 25–35 age range? Are your circumstances exactly the same as those of the 35- to 50-year-old breadwinner in his peak earning years? To do this exercise, you must factor into the equation two more elements: the mix of assets you already own and the relative security of your main source of income, most probably employment.

First, then, you'll examine your existing assets (savings deposits, GICs, stocks, bonds, Canada Savings Bonds, and so on) and categorize them into two groups: risk-free and non-risk-free. (Don't, for the moment, be concerned about the degrees of risk associated with investments in the latter category.)

As a guide, the following table sorts typical investments into the two categories:

Risk-Free Investments	*Risk Investments*
Savings deposits	Equity in real estate
GICs/term deposits	Stocks
Canada Savings Bonds	Bonds
Life insurance (cash surrender value)	Precious metals
Treasury bills	Commodities
	Mutual funds investing in any of the above

Although there is a very small element of risk associated with managers' performance, most people would probably also list money market funds on the risk-free side since they invest only in government-backed Treasury bills and top-quality bank-guaranteed deposits.

Next, determine the percentage of your total assets that each group represents.

Now, take a long, objective look at the relative security of your main income source: your job (unless you are in a small minority). Obviously, if there is a chance that your employment income may be in jeopardy, you will not want to expose investments to a high degree of risk; otherwise you could end up in double jeopardy.

Next, place yourself in one of the age categories below to ascertain a suggested appropriate level of risk. If you immediately feel uncomfortable with the suggested level, don't worry; you'll shortly have a chance to adjust it by changing your portfolio mix.

Age Group	*Risk Tolerance*
20–35	Intermediate
35–50	Intermediate/high
Over 50	Intermediate/low

Now let's go back to the matter of the security of your employment income. And let's assume that you are in the 20–35 age group, giving you an intermediate risk tolerance. That intermediate level can be achieved in several ways. In other words you can custom-tailor a risk level to suit you by simply altering the mix of assets.

For example, you could achieve a middle-of-the-road level by acquiring investments that were:

25 per cent risk-free;
50 per cent intermediate risk;
25 per cent high-risk.

But if you preferred to be more conservative, seeing some possibility that your employment income may not be secure, you might opt for:

35 per cent risk-free;
45 per cent intermediate-risk;
20 per cent high-risk.

If, on the other hand, you felt really bullish about your career prospects and wanted to adopt a more aggressive stance, you might select:

15 per cent risk-free;
25 per cent intermediate-risk;
60 per cent high-risk.

In terms of mutual funds, as you'll recall from Chapter 6, a risk rating is established by measuring how far the price of a fund moves up or down from its average or median price over a given period, usually five years. So in the context of these portfolios, you can categorize money market funds as risk-free, while all equity funds with a low variability rating would be intermediate/low-risk, those with an intermediate variability rating would be intermediate-risk, and those with a high rating would be intermediate/high-risk. Bond and mortgage funds have variability ratings which are lower than the average of low variability equity funds and thus can be categorized as low-risk. The following correlator will help you find the right funds for these categories from the presentations in the financial press.

CORRELATOR

RISK CATEGORY	VARIABILITY RATING	
	FINANCIAL POST	FINANCIAL TIMES
EQUITY FUNDS		
Intermediate/High-risk	AV +	Top 30 Percentile (High)
Intermediate-risk	AV	Mid 40 Percentile (Intermediate)
Intermediate/Low-risk	AV –	Bottom 30 Percentile (Low)
BOND & MORTGAGE FUNDS		
Low-risk	N/A	All Ratings
MONEY MARKET FUNDS		
Risk-free	N/A	N/A

The next step is to revisit your analysis of your existing asset mix and see how it compares to the mix you've now found is right for you. If you found that your existing asset mix was:

63 per cent risk-free investments;

37 per cent risk investments;

and you now determine that your custom profile *should* be:

35 per cent risk-free investments;

35 per cent intermediate-risk investments;

30 per cent high-risk investments;

you will want to use your mutual fund purchase to change the mix.

In the above case of course, you will have to convert 28 per cent or so of your risk-free investments to risk investments, split between intermediate and high-risk, as indicated. If your existing risk investments are all low-risk ones, you'll make changes here too.

Matching Objectives

By now, you know your objectives for the money you invest, e.g., long-term growth or current income. You also know your own risk profile and how to mix assets to achieve a blend suitable to your age and temperament. And, from earlier chapters in the book, you know the investment objectives of various types of funds (Chapter 2) and you know how to find and understand mutual funds' measures of risk (Chapter 6).

Now let's put all of this together and take another approach to choose various asset mixes suitable for the four investor profiles drawn in Chapter 5.

1. A 35-year-old single woman seeking growth and safety of principal

- We know that the objective of equity funds is to provide growth.
- We know that safety of principal is achieved with low-risk or risk-free investments.
- We'll assume her job is secure.
- We'll further assume that, at age 35, her investment objectives are long-term.
- We know that at age 35, her risk category should be intermediate/high. But her safe job and her age (only just inside the intermediate category), indicate she could be slightly more aggressive. However, she is concerned about safety of principal.

Thus we conclude that an appropriate investment mix might be:

15 per cent high-risk;
60 per cent intermediate-risk;
25 per cent risk free.

If we could convince her that over the 30 years between now and normal retirement age, we shall almost certainly see several market cycles, she might be prepared to be more aggressive and go for the following asset mix:

30 per cent high-risk;
50 per cent intermediate-risk;
20 per cent risk-free.

In short, the mix may be varied in several ways to suit the

individual investor. You can ensure that you will be comfortable with the mix you choose.

2. A married couple, age 25–35

In this profile about all we know is that their ages almost certainly put them in the intermediate risk tolerance category. So, to complete an examination of this couple's needs, we'll have to make some assumptions:

- they are both 26 and are expecting their first child;
- their income from employment is secure;
- their investment program is long-term;
- their existing assets are 100 per cent risk-free;
- they seek growth but are also concerned with access to their invested money in case of emergency.

An appropriate asset mix might then be:

15 per cent high-risk;
60 per cent intermediate-risk;
25 per cent low-risk or risk-free.

Or if they are more aggressive and were not planning a family for several years:

25 per cent high-risk;
60 per cent intermediate-risk;
15 per cent risk-free.

3. A man, age 35–50 in his peak earning years

In this profile, one can begin the analysis by placing him in the intermediate/high-risk category.

For the first asset mix suggestion, let's assume:

- he is 37 years old;
- his job is secure and his income is high;
- he has expressed interest in growth investments and is prepared to leave his money invested for at least the next 20 years.

It is easy to conclude that an appropriate investment mix would be:

50 per cent high-risk;
35 per cent intermediate-risk;
15 per cent risk-free.

But as he moves through the age range, he may want to reduce the overall level of risk depending upon factors such as changing circumstances of his job or the shorter period the money is intended to remain invested.

This decision to become more conservative is an important one for anyone approaching the time when they want to use their invested money for another purpose. We've learned that stock and bond investments move in cycles and more volatile investments rise and fall more than the less volatile. Thus, a gradual move at opportune times to lower-risk or risk-free investments will stabilize the value of your total investments as you near the time you need to use them for retirement income or some other purpose.

Therefore, at 50, seven years away from the date he originally set as the end of his 20-year investment term, he may prefer an investment mix of:

35 per cent high-risk;
50 per cent intermediate-risk;
15 per cent risk-free.

This approach to asset mixing allows you to be flexible and to alter your overall investment mix to suit almost any circumstance, yet maximize investment return.

For example, in this profile our man, now age 50, may have found that his income had increased more than expected and that there was no reason to change his investment mix but rather to extend his investment term to age 65 or even beyond.

A married couple over 55 and nearing retirement

For this profile, we can begin by placing them in the intermediate/low-risk category. Let's assume that:

- their temperament is such that they prefer not to take risks;
- they enjoy a high, secure household income and own their home outright;
- their objective is to accumulate assets for retirement without risking the loss of the assets they already have;
- their ages are 56.

Therefore, an appropriate investment mix could be:

50 per cent intermediate-risk;
50 per cent risk-free.

But this mix is very conservative in line with their concern about taking risks. People of this age and older are facing retirement in widely varying circumstances. Some have the prospect of retirement income from pensions which are more than adequate for their own resources to supplement pension income. Still others will depend a great deal on their own assets as the major source of retirement income.

These factors have a major impact on the investment mix decisions of people over 50 years of age.

For example, the couple whose retirement needs were more than satisfied through pensions could very easily be comfortable with an investment mix which was:
100 per cent intermediate/low.
For them, a program of investment now and well into retirement would be simply one of conserving and modestly accumulating assets.

A couple, also age 56, whose sole resources for retirement income are the assets which they have accumulated, may choose to purchase annuities. In such a case, they may start with the original investment mix suggestion for the 56-year-olds, then over the next nine years or so, up to the time they intend to retire, gradually modify the mix to eventually be 100 per cent risk-free at retirement.

Thus, at age 60, their investment mix might be:

30 per cent intermediate-risk;

70 per cent risk-free.

Then over the next five years their intermediate-risk investments could be sold when prices were high and the proceeds invested in a risk-free investment such as a money market fund where it would be available to purchase the annuities.

There are limitless scenarios for people in this and all other age categories. The key is to fully comprehend your needs and circumstances and to prepare a complementary investment mix.

It is a good idea here to try preparing some asset mix suggestions for your own needs. When you do so, complete one which would be appropriate for you now and a second one for 5 to 10 years from now, making reasonable assumptions about what your circumstances could be at that time.

Matching your needs to appropriate investments

The final step gets right down to specifics. Here, using both the data you now know about yourself and the classifications of funds according to risk in the financial press, you can now decide exactly which fund or funds you need.

The selection process is simple from here on in:

Step 1. Set out your existing asset mix.

Step 2. Write down the particular risk profile you've decided is suited to your age and temperament.

Step 3. Write down your specific objectives—growth, income, tax savings, etc.

Step 4. Keep enough aside to satisfy those short-term needs (trip, purchase, vacation, emergency fund, etc.) when you wish.

Step 5. Select specific types of funds, in appropriate risk categories and in the proportions necessary to change your existing asset mix so that it conforms to your custom profile.

Step 6. Within those categories, choose funds that have a comparably good performance record.

If we go back to our first investor profile, the 35-year-old single woman, we can follow these steps through to selection:

Step 1. We don't know her existing assets but we'll assume they're 100 per cent risk-free.

Step 2. Her risk category is intermediate but she's at the low end of the 35-50 age scale and her career looks good, so we'll adjust it to intermediate/high.

Step 3. Her objectives are growth and safety of principal.

Step 4. To cover her short-term needs, we'll assume that 10 per cent of her existing assets will suffice.

Step 5. Her suitable investment risk is:
30 per cent high-risk;
50 per cent intermediate-risk;
20 per cent risk-free.

Step 6. Using the correlator on page 124, examine the equity, bond, mortgage and money market funds listed in the financial press performance tables. For the high risk component, select from equity funds in the variability grouping labelled Average + (A +) or high, and choose from funds whose track records are comparatively good over all the periods reported.

For the intermediate-risk component, you can select from equity funds in the average or intermediate variability group. For any low-risk component, choose from equity funds in the Average – (A –) or low variability group or from bond and mortgage funds which are all low variability. For the risk-free component, choose from money market funds listed.

Influence of market conditions

As you now know well, investment markets move in cycles. You already understand that the value of income funds investing in interest-bearing securities, moves in inverse relationship to the direction of interest rates. As one goes up, the other comes down. And, of course, an equity fund's price responds to the price movement of stocks in its portfolio; as stocks trade on an exchange, their prices are primarily influenced by the supply of and demand for shares and the relative ability of companies to earn money.

As business cycles move upward, companies make more money, share prices increase, demand for stock increases, the supply of shares decreases and prices rise further. Optimism is a key motivator of everyone in such a cycle.

But if pessimism creeps in and influential people express anxiety about the short-term outlook, shares are sold, the supply of stock consequently increases while demand declines and prices fall. If underlying conditions in the economy show weakness, then the business cycle begins to move downward. In these circumstances, interest rates frequently rise initially, then start declining as recession sets in.

This brief layman's description of market movements is simply to remind you of the basics of Chapter 5, in which we explored in detail the anatomy of bulls and bears. This also seems an appropriate place to restate something else that was said in Chapter 5. Investment should be a long-term undertaking (except, of course, relatively liquid, no-cost investments such as Treasury bills and term deposits to meet short-term needs). It has been repeatedly demonstrated that trading securities for profit is not nearly as beneficial as diligently accumulating assets.

However, from time to time your changing needs will dictate changes in the asset mix of your portfolio. At such times, you will want to look at market movements in case they suggest a shift from one type of investment to another. That is the purpose of the guidelines below; we are *not* recommending that you become a practising market timer.

If interest rates decline:
- Hold money market funds
- Increase bond and mortgage funds
- Increase equity funds

If interest rates rise:
- Increase money market funds
- Decrease bond and mortgage funds
- Hold equity funds

If the business cycle turns down (recession):
- Increase money market funds (at beginning of downturn)
- Increase bond and mortgage funds (as downturn deepens)
- Decrease equity funds

If the business cycle turns up (inflation):
- Increase equity funds
- Decrease bond and mortgage funds

If the business cycle is static:
- Make no changes. Hold balance in various investment forms as dictated by your custom profile.

These are precisely the kinds of strategies that many managers of balanced funds employ. And this is perhaps an appropriate place to remind you that if your personal objectives indicate a need for both equity funds and income funds, you should consider a balanced fund. Not only will it give you the mix you need; as market conditions change, the manager will also employ suitable strategies. And you'll be saved the trouble of doing so yourself.

Whatever your choice, if you have drawn your investor profile accurately, then matched your needs and temperament to the stated investment objectives and risk profiles of various funds, and if, having bought, you regularly keep track to make sure you're still on target, we're confident that you'll be very comfortable investing, and successful to boot.

CHAPTER 8

How to Evaluate the Costs of Mutual Funds

by Peggy Waterton

In this chapter, we're going to take a close look at the final factor you'll consider when deciding whether to buy this fund or that one: the fees and other costs you may face along the way. As you know from Chapter 6, there are many other criteria you use to evaluate funds. But, all other things being equal, you will then closely examine the costs involved because they could have considerable impact on the return your money will earn, if you are not investing for the long term.

In fact, the subject is of increasing importance. Having read this far, you are already familiar with two terms: front-end load and rear-end load, or the sales charges levied respectively when you buy and when you sell. Once, they were just about all you had to be concerned with since, along with the management fee every fund charges for managing your investment, they were usually the only charges imposed. Today, however, commission and fee arrangements have become more complex, and you need to be aware of them all. Question the person from whom you're buying. Hunt through a fund's prospectus for corroboration; as you learned in Chapter 4, you won't find all costs conveniently grouped in one place.

Now let's examine all these charges one by one, starting with the sales charge, because it's still the most significant consideration.

Initial sales charge

The number of funds levying initial sales charges is declining as a proportion of the fund universe as a whole. This is because trust companies, banks and credit unions—which do not charge either front- or rear-end loads—are introducing new funds into the marketplace.

Simply stated, the sales charge is a commission or fee paid when you buy. It is not added to the cost of your purchase, as brokerage fees are. Instead, it is deducted from the amount you pay. So if you are investing $10,000 with a fund charging you 9 per cent, $900 comes off the top as a sales commission and $9,100 is invested.

The initial sales charge and the other commission arrangements described later are paid by you to the organization selling the fund. Sometimes it is the fund's principal distributor which employs its own salespeople and in the other situations it is the selling organization (a broker or mutual fund dealer) which sells the fund's shares.

Salespeople who sell mutual funds are required by law to make sure that investments purchased by their clients are suitable and are fully explained. In the course of this activity, salespeople spend considerable time explaining investment, tax implications, and risk factors, and can take much of the burden associated with examining many kinds of funds from your shoulders.

It is this sort of counsel you receive in exchange for the commission you pay as well as the ongoing opportunity to discuss the investment with your representative. You should insure that the advice you receive represents value in relation to the amount of commission you pay. If you need less advice than other prospective purchasers, then, as you'll see later, you should expect to negotiate the rate of sales charge lower. If you need a lot of advice to sort out what appears to be a daunting undertaking, expect to pay closer to top rates. If you're very sophisticated and have determined specific funds suitable to your objectives and temperament, then you should pay a much lower rate of commission (only for computing the transaction) or select from available no-load funds.

When you study the literature on mutual funds, you will often find that the sales charge is stated as "not exceeding the rates in the following table", and 9 per cent is a common maximum. In many cases the percentage may be lower—say 6.5 or 8.5—but it is invariably qualified by the words "maximum" or "up to." Two possibilities underly that qualifier.

The first is that the fund has a pre-established sliding scale of sales charge. The more you invest, the less you are charged. Assuming you make a single lump-sum purchase, for instance, here's a typical example of the commission you might pay:

Size of purchase	*Per cent sales charge*
Up to $ 9,999	8.5 per cent
$ 10,000 - $ 24,999	7.5 per cent
$ 25,000 - $ 49,999	6.0 per cent
$ 50,000 - $ 99,999	4.5 per cent
$100,000 - $199,999	3.5 per cent
$200,000 - $299,999	2.5 per cent
$300,000 - $499,999	1.5 per cent
$500,000 and over	Fully negotiable rate

The other possibility is that you may be able to negotiate the charge you will pay—and not just when you have half a million dollars to invest as in the above scale of charges.

As one example, you might sign a "letter of intent" to earn a discount on the sales charge. This letter states your intent to purchase a specified dollar amount of the fund's shares over a specified period of time. If you are later unable to complete the total purchase, you'll normally have to pay the regular sales charge on the amounts so far invested.

(In a similar vein, we should note here that according to some securities regulations, if an order is placed that qualifies for less than a 2 per cent sales charge and if that buy is redeemed within 90 days, the investor must pay the difference between the rate paid and 2 per cent to the *fund* upon early redemption. This is to prevent large investors from indulging in short-term speculation, since such speculation would involve the fund in excessive costs and be detrimental to other fundholders.)

You may also be able to negotiate a lower load if you are buying two or more funds from a fund "family" and if they total a substantial purchase. Known as 'rights of accumulation', such purchases, and even purchases of several members of the same family, can be considered together for sales charge rate determination.

Variations on the way the sales charge is levied are emerging. For instance, one fund of Mustard Seed Capital Management of Vancouver adds the sales fee to the capital invested, instead of deducting it. The fee is 10 per cent, which makes this sound like a bad deal. In fact, it is not as bad as it looks. With $10,000 available, buyer A, investing in a fund with a regular 9 per cent front-end load, actually invests $9,100. Mustard Seed's buyer B pays out $11,000 for a $10,000 investment. And the $1,000 that goes to pay the sales fee represents just under 9.1 per cent of $11,000.

Note, too, that some funds which have no initial sales charge instead charge a one-time set-up fee. This is a fixed dollar amount. Usually it represents a smaller percentage of the amount that would be charged as a commission. One fund's set-up fee, for instance, is only $5 but others range up to $100.

Other funds again charge a combination of load and set-up fee, for example up to 1 per cent plus $100.

A fund's maximum commission generally does not exceed 9 per cent. And clearly many buyers pay considerably less; a survey by The Investment Funds Institute of Canada estimates that, industry-wide, sales charges average 5 to 5.5 per cent. In any event, if you are interested in one of these funds, try to negotiate the load down; over the long haul, it could mean a difference of several thousand dollars, as we'll see shortly.

Sales charges in contractual plans

You'll pay a much higher sales charge on a fund purchase if you are buying under a contractual plan, i.e., contracting to make several deposits over a specified period of time rather than one lump-sum purchase. (You'll learn more about these plans in Chapter 9.)

What happens is that you'll pay a much higher percentage of the sales charge during the first year. Later, the percentage will drop because the total number of projected deposits are the base used to calculate the charges, and securities law limits the total overall charge to 12 per cent. Because of these higher percentages in the first year, an investor who terminates the contract early will pay a much higher overall sales charge percentage than he or she would if the plan was cancelled near its end. It is even conceivable that early cancellation of the plan and the redemption of units could mean an overall loss on the investment. Note carefully the description of these plans in Chapter 9 because understanding fully how they work is very important.

Some contractual plans have been organized differently but still work out to charge no more than an overall 12 per cent on all the instalments made.

Here, we'll assume a buyer who contracts to contribute $100 per month over 10 years (or a 120-month period) to a fund charging 9 per cent. Ahead of his or her first $100, this buyer will pay the equivalent of three contributions, or $300, none of which is invested, all of which is sales commission. Thereafter the buyer pays $9 (9 per cent) commission per contribution, but at each contribution 1/120th of that upfront sales charge is refunded to him or her. The refund equals $2.50 ($300 ÷ 120). So, in fact, $93.50 of each $100 contribution is being invested throughout the plan's duration.

Deferred sales charges

Usually identified in the funds' literature as redemption fees or contingent sales charges, these are the fees payable when redeeming your units in a fund. Deferred sales charges are a little less common than initial sales charges although they are becoming more evident, and their consequences for the investor are different.

The percentage charged as a deferred sales charge is modestly lower than those of initial sales charge: 4.5 to 7 per cent is generally the range of deferred sales charge. The important point to look for, however, is the amount that percentage is levied on. It may be levied on your purchase cost, or it may be levied on the value of your investment when you sell it—which, of course, may be higher.

For instance, if you invested a $10,000 lump sum, and if it grew at an average compound rate of 12 per cent over the next 10 years, it would by then be worth $31,058. Calculated on purchase cost, a 4.5 per cent deferred charge would amount to $450. Calculated on current value, it would be $1,398. While the current-value calculation is the one more commonly used, there may also be a provision limiting the amount to no more than 9 per cent of cost value.

Deferred sales charges are all constructed in such a way that they reduce to zero after a holding period which is generally between 6 and 9 years presently.

Here, then, is another very good reason to consider a mutual fund investment as a long-term one.

Other sales charge arrangements

A few funds charge both an initial and deferred sales charge. Typically, the fee is 3.5 per cent at both ends, with the deferred fee calculated on current value, although, again, the total initial and deferred charge usually will not exceed 9 per cent of cost value.

To see how this will work out, we'll again assume a $10,000 lump-sum investment earning an average compound rate of 12 per cent per year. The 3.5 per cent charge going in will take $350. After 10 years at 12 per cent, as we saw above, the $10,000 investment will be worth $31,058. A 3.5 per cent deferred charge would thus translate into $1,087. So this investor would pay a total charge of $1,437.

The impact of sales charge

Now let's see what impact sales charge can have on your investment over the short, medium and long term.

We've laid this out for you in tabular form below. The table shows what happens to $20,000 invested in four funds with different sales charge arrangements. Each fund is returning an average 14 per cent per year compounded annually. The dollar figures show what an investor would receive if he/she sold out at the end of the year shown in the first column.

END OF YEAR	*Fund #1* Initial sales charge 8%	*Fund #2* No load	*Fund #3* Deferred sales charge 4.5% declining	*Fund #4* Split charge— initial and on redemption 3.5%
1	$20,976	$22,800	$21,774	$21,232
2	$23,913	$25,992	$24,952	$24,204
4	$31,077	$33,779	$32,428	$31,496
6	$40,388	$43,899	$43,021	$41,262
8	$52,488	$57,051	$56,481	$53,955
10	$68,213	$74,144	$74,144	$70,449
15	$131,338	$142,758	$142,758	$136,662

Notes

1. The deferred sales charges in Funds #3 and #4 are calculated on current values.
2. Fund #3's declining charge is applied as follows: year 1, 4.5 per cent; year 2 and year 4, 4 per cent; year 6, 2 per cent; year 8, 1 per cent; 10th and subsequent years, nil.
3. Fund #4's split charge of 3.5 per cent must not total more than 9 per cent of purchase value, or $1,800. The initial fee is $700, so the deferred charge cannot exceed $1,100. That maximum is levied at the end of the 4th and all subsequent years.

Management fees

All mutual funds charge management fees. The managers must, after all, be paid for their efforts to grow our money, and also be reimbursed for the costs they incur in so doing. Typically, the annual management fee charged ranges from 0.5 to 2 per cent of the total assets under management.

These fees are charged directly to the fund. In other words, you will not suddenly find yourself facing a bill for them. They do, of course, have an impact on your investment's return. A fund whose managers are achieving a 15 per cent return on assets and receiving 1.5 per cent of that return in fees is actually showing its investors a net return of 13.5 per cent. This latter, incidentally, is the return which the fund will show in its sales literature and other documents, and the one which the financial press will publish in its surveys. In other words, the stated returns are always net of management fees.

Occasionally, these fees are on a sliding scale, the percentage dropping as the fund's asset pool increases.

Some fund surveys, you will find, show the funds' management expense ratio. This is calculated by adding the dollar amount of the annual management fees and the dollar amount of the legal and audit fees, and other expenses, and expressing this total as a percentage of the average net asset value of the fund during the fiscal year.

As an example let's look at a statement from the hypothetical ABC Fund:

Management fees incurred by the fund ...	$342,278.00
Expenses incurred by the fund	24,440.00
Total of management fees and other expenses	366,718.00
The average net asset value of the fund ..	$20,000,000.00
Management Expense Ratio	1.83%

The management expense ratio for the last five years must be set out in the fund's prospectus and the annual financial statements.

Management fees are used to pay the management company for its portfolio management services, general management services and expenses which the management company pays on behalf of the fund.

Distribution fees

These are frequently charged by funds that have a deferred sales charge structure. They may also be identified as sales administration fees. Distribution fees exist to provide some of the money to pay commissions to salespeople who sell such funds. Because purchasers pay no initial sales charge, the principal distributor pays salespeople and recovers the commissions partly from the distribution fee and partly from the deferred sales charge. They are typically around 1 per cent of the fund's net asset value and, like management fees, they're charged to the fund, not to the investor's account.

Service fees

These are fees which are paid to salespeople for providing continuous service to clientele of the fund. Sometimes called 'trailer fees', they supplement the income of distributors which otherwise would only be paid for their work from the one-time initial sales charge.

Most salespeople are happy to provide ongoing service to their clients after they have sold a plan. Their incentive is a happy customer who may buy again and who may refer new clients to them. Recognizing that sales organizations incur costs in connection with the service function, some fund organizations have arranged to pay the service fee out of the management fee income they receive.

While no separate charge to the fund or investors' accounts is made, such fees will impact on investors if management fees need to be increased to accommodate payment of a service fee. Otherwise it is simply an additional cost of the management company.

Administrative charges

Administrative charges are generally found in special plans that require complex computer systems or other unique transaction services.

Such charges are typical in contractual accumulation plans and systematic withdrawal plans which require monthly processing and tracking of payment numbers, post-dated cheques (or pre-authorized payments), monthly redemption cheque, etc. Usually the charge is $1.50 per month and is paid by each investor.

Money market funds which allocate income to fundholders daily also charge for additional administrative services and the amount charged to each investor is typically $1.50 per month.

Transfer fees

Perhaps you'll want to stay with the same fund organization but switch to a different fund in the group. There will normally be a charge, albeit not a large one, usually an amount up to 2 per cent of the capital involved, or a flat $10–$15 conversion fee.

Termination fees

This fee is usually found in a no-load fund and is paid by investors to cover the expense of administrative work involved in closing the account. This fee is charged to an investor who opts out of a contractual plan. You'll find more about this in the next chapter.

Retirement savings plans

All you need to know here is that special services of an RSP trustee are required to assure Revenue Canada that the contributions will remain tax sheltered and not be used directly by the investor. RSP trustees report the amounts of annual contributions to Revenue Canada for all deposits they receive as trustee for the contributor. They are also responsible for the direct transfers to other trustees as requested by planholders and for reporting terminations of RSPs. Fees of RSP trustees include both an annual charge and a termination fee, both taken from the planholders' accounts.

Pulling it all together

The whole question of fees must now seem to be almost overwhelming. The confusion in terms; the number of different fees, commissions or charges; the comparative impact of paying commissions on purchase or redemption; cost of contractual plans versus voluntary plans—all these are some of the factors which must have evoked the title of this book.

The appraisal of cost can be simplified if these commissions, fees and charges are divided into three main categories: sales charges, management fees and other charges. Thus we will be able to compare costs of similar type.

Sales charges

These costs are only for the distribution of the fund's shares or units and are paid to salespeople and the organizations which employ them. If you purchase a fund which is sold by salespeople and pay a sales charge of any kind make certain that you receive, in return, advice and service which you judge commensurate with the amount you pay. Here is a brief summary of types of sales charge:

• Initial sales charge is a percentage of the amount originally invested which starts at 9 per cent in smaller amounts and declines as the size of your purchase increases. Frequently this charge is negotiable so that you and the salesperson can decide on a rate that is appropriate for the time involved in his or her advisory function. You may also reduce the rate of sales charge by signing a letter of intent to purchase a large total investment over time or by establishing rights of accumulation where purchases of several related people can be considered together.

• Deferred sales charge is similar to initial sales charge in that its rate varies in relation to the amount of the investment but it is not charged until redemption. Typically, deferred sales charges decline in rate each year you hold the investment without selling, eventually being eliminated. Some funds charge the fee on market value of the investment redeemed and others charge on the redemption's cost value.

• Contractual plans have a unique sales charge designed to compensate salespeople more appropriately for the time taken to explain the investment than if they received only the initial sales charge on each purchase. In a $50 monthly plan in which one-half of the first year's payments went to commission, the sales charge of $300 would go to the salesperson and his or her employer instead of $54 (12 × 9 per cent of $50). Such a sale could typically take four hours or so. Remember too that in the second and subsequent years, sales charge is considerably lower than the normal 9 per cent so that over the plan your cost is an average of 9 per cent. Plans which call for a deposit initially of three instalments which all go to commission produce the same net result—the salesperson gets more in the beginning and less later on averaging out to a 9 per cent average cost to you. Because both these arrangements involve a higher sales charge at the beginning of the plan, or the front end, they're commonly called front-end load plans.

• Distribution fees are charged, not to you but to the fund in which you invest. They are used to compensate salespeople who sell funds which have a deferred sales charge and no initial commission.

• Service fees are paid by management companies out of their management fees to sales organizations to compensate them for costs in providing ongoing service to their clients. This should not affect individual shareholders unless the management fee is raised to accommodate payment of the service fee.

Management fees

For the portfolio management duties and for the responsibilities in the general management of a fund's affairs, a fund pays the manager or trustee a management fee. Generally, this fee does not exceed two per cent and can be considerably lower. Some managers or trustees undertake to pay all the fund's expenses out of an overall management fee and others charge a fee only for their services with the fund paying its own expenses. The prospectus or simplified prospectus describes this fully.

Other charges

RSP trustee fees, termination fees, services charges in systematic withdrawal plans and accumulation plans and money market fund monthly invoice fees are all typical of these other 'user' charges. They are simply compensation for specific services you may request.

No-load funds

In discussing charges, it is also important to assess funds without sales charges—no-load funds.

No-load funds are available from the management company or distributor which is affiliated with the fund(s). If you wish to discuss no-load funds, you will likely get your information from a salaried employee of the firm. Because no-load funds are proprietary to the company offering them, you will only get information about the fund(s) offered by that company from their employees.

The important thing to remember here is that because you do not pay a commission to a salesperson, there is no one to investigate which funds may be suitable for you. You must do this work on your own. Chapters 7 and 9 will be helpful in that undertaking. As well, it is your responsibility to do the ongoing monitoring of your investments as is described in Chapters 5 and 7.

Costs are an important consideration to every investor and are not just to be avoided. To be satisfied you should make sure that you receive value for the costs you face and that is probably most important when it comes to sales charge. Find out first what the salesperson will do for you and how much will be charged. That will help you evaluate its worth.

CHAPTER 9

How to Buy and Sell Mutual Funds

by Keith A. Douglas

By now, you have all the tools you need in order to find the fund or funds that best suit your financial goals, personal circumstances and temperament, and how to recognize when it might subsequently be wise to consider redeeming your units, perhaps to move to another fund. Now, we'll take a look at the mechanics of buying and selling mutual fund investments: whom you buy from, how the transaction is completed, the various purchase options open to you and so on.

Along the way, you will also learn about a very useful strategy for investing in mutual funds that will save you from an emotional trap many investors fall into. And we'll discuss another investment strategy that you might be well advised *not* to use.

Who sells mutual funds?

To find an answer, we must first go back to Chapter 8. There, you learned that funds fall into one of two broad categories: those that impose sales charges or commissions and those that do not.

In the case of no-load funds that do not impose sales charges, sales are generally "proprietary" — that is, they are made by employees of the company that sponsors the fund. Almost all funds sponsored by banks, trust companies and credit unions fall into this category. A few fund management companies also have no-load funds which they sell both direct to the public and through investment dealers (whom they compensate for sales made).

In the case of funds which impose sales charges, the fund typically uses (and rewards with commissions) an intermediary to sell units. That intermediary might be a proprietary distribution force it controls, an independent mutual fund dealer or a securities firm. You will hence be buying from a captive mutual fund salesperson, an independent mutual fund salesperson, or a stockbroker's sales representative.

Funds sponsored by the financial institutions are the most accessible of all; in most cases, you can buy them at any branch of the institution. If you were interested in discussing a fund purchase with an intermediary, you would find mutual fund salespersons prepared to come to your home or office. Stock brokers are easily accessible by telephone but you'll likely have to visit their office, at least for the first interview. For all fund companies, you will find head offices, addresses and telephone numbers in the Directory of Funds that starts on page 161 of this book.

Completing a purchase

Securities laws require that any person who sells a mutual fund must be satisfied that the particular fund is suitable for the purchaser. You will therefore be asked to complete an application form on which you'll provide sufficient information about yourself to allow suitability to be reasonably determined.

Once the application is complete and you have received the prospectus and other necessary information, you provide a cheque payable to the fund or to the dealer if you are purchasing through a representative. You should obtain a receipt for your payment. Shortly after your purchase is processed, you can expect to receive official confirmation from the fund. These confirmations of transactions are your record of purchases, since funds generally do not issue share certificates, so it is important to keep them somewhere safely. (Except for annual statements of account and for certificates which are seldom issued, confirmations are the only record of transactions, including especially dividends/trustee fee deductions.)

Rights of withdrawal and rescission

You signed an agreement to purchase, and now you are having second thoughts. Can you change your mind?

Securities legislation in Canada establishes certain rights for mutual fund investors to opt out of their purchase. In some jurisdictions, you are entitled to withdraw from your investment and receive all of your money back, both the sales charge and the cost of the shares or units. To exercise this right you must give written notice of intention to withdraw no later than 48 hours after receipt of the prospectus (in some provinces) or after receipt of the confirmation of purchase (in other provinces). In addition, several provinces permit you to rescind your purchase if it does not exceed a specified amount (usually $50,000), provided notice to that effect is given within 48 hours after receipt of the confirmation of purchase. However, this right of rescission only permits you to recover the lesser of the price you paid for the shares or units and the value of the shares or units at the time of exercise of the right of rescission. If the units or shares have declined in price since you purchased them, you will lose some money. The dealer from whom you purchased the shares or units must also reimburse to you the sales charge you paid. Purchasers under contractual plans have the same right of rescission provided they give notice within 60 days after the first payment is made under the plan.

In most provinces,you have the right to seek damages or to recover the cost of your investment if the prospectus contained a misrepresentation or, in some provinces, if the prospectus was not delivered to either you or the dealer from whom you purchased the shares or units. No action to enforce these rights may be commenced later than a specified period which generally ranges from one and one-half years to three years after the date of your purchase.

If the value of the fund's units has fallen since you made the purchase, the mutual fund is required to refund to you only that lower current value, so you may lose money in exercising the right. If you have paid a front-end load, however, that must be returned to you in full.

Licensing requirements

People from whom you may buy mutual funds offer securities. Thus they are subject to Canada's securities laws. Until recently, employees of banks, trust companies and credit unions in Ontario were exempt from licencing procedures. However, starting in 1988, everyone who sells a mutual fund in the province must be registered with the provincial securities commission. To be eligible for registration, an applicant must have passed a specific licensing course.

At publication, Saskatchewan was about to formalize rules for employees of banks, trust companies and credit unions. As well, the institutions themselves have, in many cases, voluntarily registered their employees in all provinces, believing universal registration would be a national practice eventually. In any event, you are well advised to ask if the person discussing mutual funds with you is registered with a securities commission and, if not, to ask to speak to someone who is registered.

In addition to this registration and its concomitant education standards, securities laws also provide that procedures be in place to ensure that each registered person complies with all the relevant securities laws.

Ongoing procedures

Now that you have bought a mutual fund, you can expect to receive certain documents regularly.

All funds must send annual audited financial statements to all their shareholders or unitholders within 140 days of the end of the fiscal year. In addition, unaudited semi-annual financial statements are required to be delivered to fund owners and many funds provide quarterly reports of both financial and investment information. All of these reports are important to you, especially since you are actively managing your investment.

All mutual funds organized as corporations are required by law to hold annual meetings of shareholders in the same way as are industrial companies. The business on the agenda of fund annual meetings is very similar to that of their industrial counterparts but, since the business of a mutual fund is investment management, most of the meeting is about the investment strategy of the portfolio managers.

If you are unable to attend, your vote may be exercised by proxy. As a shareholder, you are entitled to satisfactory accountability from management. The vote to which you are also entitled should be cast to register your approval or disapproval — it counts.

Funds which are organized as trusts do not hold annual meetings because trust law gives responsibility for your interests to the fund's trustees. While there are some matters over which you have no control, securities rules require special meetings of unitholders before certain changes to fund operations can be undertaken. For example, changing the investment objectives of the fund may not be done without unitholder approval. These rules for special meetings also apply to mutual fund corporations.

Purchase plans

In earlier chapters, you have seen frequent references to lump-sum purchases and contractual plans. Now we'll explore these various purchase methods a little more closely.

Lump-sum purchase

This is exactly what the name implies. You invest a single sum of money. You will probably have to meet a minimum requirement: $250–$1,000 in the case of most funds, or up to $5,000 for money market funds.

If you subsequently decide to add other lump sums to the first, you may not be subject to any minimum requirement. If there is one, it will be much lower than the initial amount—typically $25 to $100.

Accumulation plans

These plans allow you to buy mutual funds by making regular payments of smaller amounts over a given period. There are two basic types. In a *contractual plan*, you contract to complete the plan over a given period, say 10 or 15 years, by paying fixed monthly instalments. In a *voluntary plan*, you also make instalment payments, but you are free to change the size of your payments at any time, or to stop them altogether.

There is nothing to say that you can't stop making payments on a contractual plan. But in these plans, remember, the sales charge structure is such that you pay a large commission in the beginning but less later on. This means that should you cancel your plan after the first year but before it is completed, you will end up having paid a disproportionately high average sales charge on the instalments you made. If you decide not to rescind a contractual plan within the permitted time period, it is to your advantage to complete it so you can average out the sales charge. Besides, there are other benefits such as completion insurance if you die or become disabled, partial withdrawal privileges which allow you to redeem some of your investment temporarily, then replace it at no sales charge, and so on.

Voluntary plans are simply a method of buying mutual fund shares or units with regular instalments of as little as $25.00 monthly. There is no contract and there are no special sales charge structures. There are also no special options in voluntary plans as are found in most contractual plans.

Both voluntary and contractual plans allow you to accumulate assets through an important investment strategy known as dollar-cost averaging.

Dollar-cost averaging

This strategy involves the regular investment of a fixed amount in shares of mutual funds whose value fluctuates and has the objective of lowering the average cost of your accumulated shares. Let's see how it works.

Assume that you have contracted to make monthly contributions of $100. Assume, further, that at each purchase date the value of the fund's shares or units has changed. At the first purchase date, the price stood at $12, so your $100 bought 8.333 shares, but by the fourth purchase date the price had slid to $9, so this contribution bought 11.111 shares.

In other words, when the value is high, you buy fewer shares. And when it declines, you buy more.

So here's the first benefit associated with dollar-cost averaging. When market values decline, many investors stop buying; it is human nature not to want to be associated with a failing proposition. Conversely, when things appear to be on an upward swing, it is human nature to jump in and buy. But this is not good investor behavior; we should buy low and sell high. In your accumulation plan, of course, you are buying at all times. *But you are buying more shares when the price is right.*

There's a second and equally important benefit. Because you are buying more shares or units when the price dips down, the average cost of all the shares you have bought is less than the average of the prices of those shares when they were bought. And since market prices tend to rise over the long term, your lower average cost will enhance your profit and will also put you in line for a capital gain sooner.

To illustrate this, let's assume that you make just six of those monthly $100 payments. (Your plan will probably extend over a far longer period, but a six-month illustration will serve our purpose.) The table below shows you what might happen during that period. The third and fourth columns show the month-by-month relationship between the accumulated cost of your investment and its total market value. Even though the price six months later is the same as when you began, you have achieved a gain of $54.72 or more than 9 per cent. Had you made a single lump sum investment of $600.00 in month 1, its value would still be

Month	NAVPS	Number of shares bought	Total cost of investment	Total value of investment
#1	$12	8.333	$100	$100.00
#2	$11	9.091	$100	$191.66
#3	$10	10.000	$300	$274.24
#4	$ 9	11.111	$400	$346.82
#5	$13	7.692	$500	$600.00
#6	$12	8.333	$600	$654.72
	Average of prices $11.16	Total number of shares 54.560		Average cost per share $10.997

$600.00 six months later. Looking at the example another way, the 54.560 shares you have accumulated cost you $600.00 or an average of $10.99 per share but the average of the prices paid is $11.16. That's how dollar-cost averaging works—it gives you an average cost weighted in favor of the lower prices paid.

Systematic Withdrawal Plans

Anyone needing periodic income, say monthly, may decide to invest a substantial sum in mutual funds, then make arrangements to sell some units each month to provide part of the income. For example, you purchase $200,000 of shares and ask for a 12 per cent withdrawal plan so that you will receive a monthly cheque of $2,000.00. Every month, sufficient shares or units will be sold at market value to produce the $2,000.00 required.

The value of the original investment will fluctuate up and down and at each valuation date the new price will reflect accrued income as well as market gains or losses. At least annually the fund will distribute dividend income and, likely, capital gains, both of which will be reinvested and added to your account.

If the combination of dividend income, capital gains and market value appreciation works out to be 12 per cent of your investment, your systematic withdrawal will not eat into your original capital. If it is more, your investment will grow; if it is less, the size of your investment will shrink.

Some systematic withdrawal plans charge a small administrative fee to send the monthly cheque.

Most funds allow you to withdraw a fixed percentage, a fixed amount or an amount adjusted to life expectancy for those in retirement.

Leveraging

You have just learned about one of the best strategies for buying mutual funds. Now we should talk about another strategy—this time, one which you should approach with extreme caution and one which many investors should not use at all, in fact.

Leveraging simply means borrowing money, adding it to your own and making an investment with the total. The amount you owe remains static, or is reduced by repayments, while the total investment grows in value. So the total growth belongs to you. In this way you increase the rate at which your own money can grow.

For example, instead of investing $20,000, you decide to borrow $80,000 and invest a total of $100,000. The investment then grows by 20 per cent to $120,000. You still owe $80,000, so your interest in the total investment is now $40,000. That's not a 20 per cent gain. Leverage has increased the gain on your investment to 100 per cent. Add to this the advantage of being able to deduct some of the loan interest from taxable income (unless this is an RRSP investment you are making; under tax reform, interest paid on loans taken out to make an RRSP contribution is no longer deductible.) And you won't pay tax on your first $100,000 of capital gain. Leveraging sounds very attractive, doesn't it?

Well, there's another side to the story. Just as gains on your investment can be magnified by leverage, so can losses. Let's go back to that $80,000 you borrowed to add to your $20,000. Now let's suppose that the entire $100,000 investment *declines* in value by 20 per cent. In other words, it is now worth $80,000 —precisely the amount you owe. Your own $20,000 has been wiped out.

If mutual fund shares bought with a leverage loan must be pledged to the lender as security, another potential problem exists. If the investment declines in value, the lender may now feel that the loan is too large a percentage of the total investment. Now, one of three things must be done. The borrower must pay down the loan. Or the borrower must come up with additional collateral security. Or the lender will sell the security in order to pay off the loan.

And all these gloomy prospects must be faced at the very time you're watching your investment decline.

If you really believe leveraging is for you, obey these rules:

- don't borrow to invest when prices are high—it's much safer when markets are relatively low;

• keep a sufficiently large financial cushion to see you through any declines. Also make sure your cash flow will permit you to continue loan payments;
• avoid using other collateral, and especially a home—you may find yourself *without* the investment and *with* a mortgage;
• consider carefully the tax consequences—under tax reform, exempt capital gains must now be reduced by interest expense deducted from taxable income;
• borrow only a small percentage of the total investment. Stock exchange and investment dealer rules prohibit loans by brokers of more than 50 per cent of the value of stock being purchased. It's a good rule for everyone else too.

Buying on margin is similar to leveraging. The only difference is the loan is provided by a stockbrokerage firm which accepts the investment made as collateral. In a declining market, you face exactly the same risks as those outlined above. You'll have to pay down, find more collateral or see your investments sold. It's worth noting that many of those who lost their shirts after Black Monday in October 1987 did so because they had bought stock on margin and had to stand by and watch their investments being sold to honor their debts.

How to sell mutual fund shares

To sell stocks or bonds, you must find someone who wants to buy. Mutual funds, as you know, are unique in that they repurchase shares from you at their current market value whenever you wish. Most funds value their assets daily, others do so weekly and some value only once a month. Real property funds normally determine value once a quarter because the value of real estate doesn't change a great deal over shorter periods.

The process by which a fund repurchases your shares is known as a redemption. You need only advise the fund, in writing, that you wish to redeem all or part of your holding.

Your redemption request will be processed at the next price calculated after your request is received. If the fund is valued daily, the price you receive will be the one calculated at the end of the day your request arrives. If the fund is valued every Friday and your request arrives on Tuesday, it will be processed at the price struck next Friday.

Some funds, especially those valued monthly or quarterly, require advance notice of your redemption. For instance, if 10 days' notice is required, you must make sure that the fund receives your request at least 10 days before the next valuation date, otherwise it will be held over until the one following. Fund prospectuses set out these requirements in detail.

You must make a redemption request in exactly the same name as that in which the fund shares or units are registered. If the units are held in the name of John George Smith, you should not request redemption as J.G. Smith.

Special rules apply to accounts registered in the names of more than one person, in the name of a corporation, in the name of one person in trust for another, in the name of the beneficial owner's nominee or in the name of a deceased person. If you're transacting a redemption in any of these special cases, check in advance with the fund to make sure you will have available the necessary documentation.

Some funds will allow you to make redemptions by telephone. In this case, the necessary documentation is set up when you open the account. You are assigned a special identification code to provide when telephoning a redemption request. The proceeds will then be sent directly to your account.

Securities laws provide that a redemption cheque must be sent out within seven days of the fund's next valuation date, provided the necessary redemption documentation has been submitted to the fund. Investment dealers commonly pay redemption proceeds within five business days of receiving a request. (The dealers are then reimbursed by the fund.)

RRSP redemptions

Because of the special tax status of RRSPs, these redemptions —whether made to withdraw funds or to transfer them, still tax-sheltered, into another RRSP—must be made through the trustee of the plan. You, however, send your request to the fund in the usual way. If you are making a withdrawal or deregistering a plan entirely, the trustee must first deduct withholding tax and remit it to Revenue Canada. On amounts up to $5,000 the tax rate is 10 per cent, on amounts up to $15,000 it is 20 per cent, and on amounts above $15,000 it is 30 per cent. The trustee also may deduct a small termination charge, typically $25–$50, then pays the balance to you. You will also receive a T4RSP reporting slip to be included with your tax return.

If you are transferring to another trustee, you are required to complete with the new trustee a T2033 form, which authorizes the release of the funds to the new trustee.

RRSP rollovers

If your RRSP investments are still intact at retirement time, you have the option of rolling them over into Registered Retirement Income Funds or selling them and buying annuities with the proceeds so that the capital remains tax-sheltered and you pay tax only on the income from these new plans as you receive it.

Mutual funds are among the investments eligible for RRIFs. The procedure is simple; having chosen the kind of RRIF payment structure you want, you merely sign an authorization form you'll get from the financial institution or mutual fund company you have invested with.

Transfers

You may decide to switch—to move from one mutual fund to another in the same "family". You need only to send a request to the fund management company or financial institution, asking that your investment be transferred. As you saw in Chapter 8, fees will be minimal so long as you stay with the same fund family.

When you want to transfer to a fund sponsored by another company or institution, you'll have to request a redemption from the first fund and complete an application for the new one. As you saw in Chapter 8, such a transaction could expose you to sales fees again.

The best strategy of all

In this last chapter we've covered the mechanics of buying, modifying and selling mutual fund investments. And we've talked a little about strategies.

But the principal strategic approach for the long term is: be an accumulator of assets, not a trader of securities. The simple approach of making regular purchases of mutual funds, or dollar-cost averaging, has proven over and over again to be more profitable than any attempt to time the purchase and sale of securities to coincide with the right market swings.

However, even though professional managers invest on your behalf when you buy into a mutual fund, you now know, after reading this book, that you can't just sit back and wait for the money to roll in. There are still certain things that you must do.

In summary, you will:

- keep your investments in tune with your objectives;
- keep your eye on your ultimate goal—don't be distracted;
- avoid situations where some outside factor (i.e., a loan) may make you sell when you'd rather not;
- keep a balance of investments or financial assets, adjusting it periodically to keep you on track toward your investment goal;
- accumulate assets for the best long-term result and avoid short-term trading.

Mutual funds provide many people with an opportunity they may not otherwise have: to invest in stocks, bonds, mortgages, real estate and many other vehicles. This book has given you all the tools you need to select and purchase the fund or funds that are most appropriate for you, and to take care of those aspects of your investment's ongoing management which are your responsibility. Use these tools and you will enhance your chances of seeing your money grow substantially. You will also discover the satisfaction of making the most informed decisions possible. It's *fun* to be in charge.

We expect you to enjoy exercising the knowledge you now have. And, of course, you have our very best wishes for a long and prosperous future as an investor!

APPENDIX I

DIRECTORY OF FUNDS

Adapted with the approval and permission of The Financial Post Company Limited from *Survey of Funds* (Dec 31, 1987 Report), published quarterly by The Financial Post Information Service.

AGF Management Limited (416) 367-1900
50th Flr., Toronto-Dominion Bank Tower
M5K 1E9

AGF Hi-Tech	(Int'l Equity)
AGF Japan	(Special)
AGF Money Market	(Fixed Income)
AGF Option	(Int'l Equity)
AGF Pfd.	(Preferred Stock)
AGF Special	(U.S. Equity)
AGF Global Gov't Bond	(Fixed Income)
American Growth	(U.S. Equity)
Canadian Gas & Energy	(Cdn. Equity)
Cdn Security Growth	(Cdn. Equity)
Canadian Trusteed	(Fixed Income)
Corporate Investors	(Cdn. Equity)
Corporate Inv Stock	(Cdn. Equity)
Growth Equity	(Cdn. Equity)
TD's Greenline Cdn Index	(Cdn. Equity)
TD's Greenline US Index	(Cdn. Equity)

AIC Group (519) 578-6760
Ste. 901, 101 Frederick St.
Kitchener, Ontario
N2H 6R2

A I C Advantage	(Cdn. Equity)

AMD Funds (416) 864-8080
3rd Floor, 145 King St. West
Toronto, Ontario
M5H 3T7

AMD Dividend	(Preferred Stock)
AMD Fixed Income	(Fixed Income)
AMD Money Market	(Fixed Income)
AMD American Blue Chip	(U.S. Equity)
AMD Canadian Blue Chip	(Cdn. Equity)
AMD U.S. Dollar Money Market	(Fixed Income)

Alliance Mutual Life Insurance Co. (514) 284-3838
680 Sherbrooke St. West
Montreal, Quebec
H3A 2S6

Alliance	(Cdn. Equity)

Allied Group (416) 869-7327
Ste. 501, 8 King St. East
Toronto, Ontario
M5C 1B5

Allied Canadian	(Cdn. Equity)
Allied Dividend	(Preferred Stock)
Allied Income	(Fixed Income)
Allied International	(Int'l Equity)
Allied Money	(Fixed Income)

Altamira Management Ltd. (416) 971-9291
20 Queen St. West
Toronto, Ontario
M5H 3R3

Altamira	(Fixed Income)

Blondeau and Company (514) 288-1600
Ste. 1600, 425 Blvd. de Maisonneuve W.
Montreal, Quebec
H3A 3G5

Fonds des Professionels B	(Balanced)
Fonds des Professionels C	(Fixed Income)

Bolton Tremblay Funds Inc. (416) 595-5200
Ste. 1040, 70 University Ave.
Toronto, Ontario
M5J 2M9

B Tremblay Int'l	(Int'l Equity)
B Tremblay Money	(Fixed Income)
B Tremblay Pref Income	(Preferred Stock)
Canada Cumulative	(Cdn. Equity)
Planned Resources	(Cdn. Equity)
Taurus	(Indicators)

CGF Fund Management Inc. (416) 591-6000
Ste. 800, 70 University Ave.
Toronto, Ontario
M5J 2M5

CGF 4000	(Cdn. Equity)
CGF Venture	(Cdn. Equity)
International Growth	(Int'l Equity)

CSA Management Ltd. (416) 865-0326
1204 IBM Tower, P.O. Box 68, T-D Centre
Toronto, Ontario
M5K 1E7

Goldfund	(Special)
Goldtrust	(Special)

Calvin Bullock, Ltd. (514) 866-5421
Ste. 2960, 630 Dorchester Blvd. W.
Montreal, Quebec
H3B 1X1

Bullock American	(U.S. Equity)
Bullock Dividend	(Pref. Stock)
Bullock Income	(Fixed Income)
Canadian Investment	(Cdn. Equity)

Canada Life Assurance Company, The (416) 597-1456
330 University Ave.
Toronto, Ontario
M5G 1R8

Canada Life E.2	(Cdn. Equity)
Canada Life S.19	(Fixed Income)
Canada Life S.29	(Fixed Income)
Canada Life S.35	(Balanced)
Canada Life S.9	(Cdn. Equity)
Canada Life S34	(U.S. Equity)

Canada Trust Company (416) 361-8411
15th Floor, 320 Bay St.
Toronto, Ontario
M5H 2P6

Canada Trust Equity	(Cdn. Equity)
Canada Trust Income	(Fixed Income)
Canada Trust Mortgage	(Fixed Income)
Canada Tr N American	(U.S. Equity)
Canada Trust RSP Equity	(Cdn. Equity)
Canada Trust RSP Income	(Fixed Income)

Canadian Anaesthetists' Society (416) 923-1449
Ste. 904, 94 Cumberland St.
Toronto, Ontario
M5R 1A3

Cdn Anaesthetists	(Cdn. Equity)

Canadian Dental Service Plans Inc. (416) 497-7117
Ste. 600, 2 Lansing Square
Willowdale, Ontario
M2J 4Z3

CDA Balanced	(Balanced)
CDA Common Stock	(Cdn. Equity)
CDA Fixed Income	(Fixed Income)
CDA Money Market	(Fixed Income)

Canadian General Life Insurance (416) 528-6766
120 King St. West
Hamilton, Ontario
L8N 3P6

Cdn. General Life A	(Cdn. Equity)
Cdn. General Life B	(Fixed Income)
Cdn. General Life C	(Fixed Income)

Canadian Imperial Bank of Commerce (416) 784-8183
Commerce Court West
Toronto, Ontario
M5L 1A2

CIBC Mortgage Investment	(Fixed Income)

Canadian Medical Association (613) 731-4552
MD Management Ltd.
CMA House
P.O. Box 8650
Ottawa, Ontario
K1G 0G8

*CMA Investment	(Cdn. Equity)
*CMA S-T Deposit	(Fixed Income)
*MD Growth Investments	(Int'l Equity)
*MD Realty A	(Special)

*Available to Canadian Medical Association members only.

Central Group Ltd., The (416) 648-2025
P.O. Box 7320
Ancaster, Ontario
L9G 3N6

All-Cdn Compound	(Cdn. Equity)
All-Cdn Dividend	(Cdn. Equity)
All-Cdn Revenue	(Fixed Income)
Natural Resources	(Cdn. Equity)
Univest Growth	(Cdn. Equity)

Central Trust Company (902) 422-1331
Box 3410—5414 Spring Garden Rd.
Halifax, Nova Scotia
B3J 3J1

Central Money Market	(Fixed Income)
Central Tr Mortgage	(Fixed Income)

Century DJ Fund (416) 860-0495
P.O. Box 449
2 First Canadian Place
Toronto, Ontario
M5X 1J7

Century D.J. Fund	(U.S. Equity)

Citadel General Assurance Co., The (416) 928-8661
12th Floor
1075 Bay Street
Toronto, Ontario
M5J 2W5

Citadel Life	(Cdn. Equity)

Confederation Life Insurance Company (416) 967-8437
321 Bloor Street East
Toronto, Ontario
M4W 1H1

Confed Dolphin	(Cdn. Equity)
Confed Life A	(Cdn. Equity)
Confed Life B	(Cdn. Equity)
Confed Life C	(Fixed Income)

Co-operative Trust Company of Canada (306) 244-1900
333 Third Ave. North
Saskatoon, Saskatchewan
S7K 2N2

Co-op Trust Growth	(Cdn. Equity)
Co-op Tr Income	(Fixed Income)

Crown Life Insurance Company (416) 928-5763
120 Bloor St. E.
Toronto, Ontario
M4W 1B8

Crown Life (CCIFA)	(Cdn. Equity)
Crown Life Balanced	(Balanced)
Crown Life Bond	(Fixed Income)
Crown Life Commitment	(Cdn. Equity)
Crown Life Equity	(Cdn. Equity)
Crown Life Foreign Equity	(Cdn. Equity)
Crown Life Mortgage	(Fixed Income)
Crown Life Short Term	(Fixed Income)

Cundill Group, The (604) 685-4231
1200, 1100 Melville St.
Vancouver, B.C.
V6C 4A6

Cundill Security	(Cdn. Equity)
Cundill Value	(U.S. Equity)

Dixon Krogseth Ltd. (604) 684-8541
Ste. 2660
1066 W. Hastings St.
Vancouver, B.C.
V6E 3X1

Dixon Krogseth Enterprise	(Cdn. Equity)
DK All Seasons	(Balanced)
DK American	(U.S. Equity)

Domequity & Growth Calgary	(403) 262-0100
1200, 205-5th Ave. S.W.	
Calgary, Alberta	
T2P 4B9	
Domequity Growth	(Cdn. Equity)
Dynamic Funds Management Ltd.	(416) 363-5621
6 Adelaide St. E.	
Toronto, Ontario	
M5C 1H6	
Dynamic American	(U.S. Equity)
Dynamic Dividend	(Pref. Stock)
Dynamic Canada	(Cdn. Equity)
Dynamic Global	(Int'l Equity)
Dynamic Income	(Fixed Income)
Dynamic Mgd. Portfolio	(Balanced)
Dynamic Precious Metal	(Special)
Dynamic Savings	(Fixed Income)
Eaton Group, The	(416) 343-4954
595 Bay Street	
Toronto, Ontario	
M5G 2C6	
Viking Canadian	(Cdn. Equity)
Viking Commonwealth	(Int'l Equity)
Viking Dividend	(Pref. Stock)
Viking Growth	(U.S. Equity)
Viking Income	(Fixed Income)
Viking International	(Int'l Equity)
Elliott & Page Limited	(416) 365-8300
Ste. 1120	
120 Adelaide St. W.	
Toronto, Ontario	
M5H 1V1	
Elliott & Page Money Fund	(Fixed Income)
NAL Investor Bluechip	(Cdn. Equity)
NAL Investor Bond	(Fixed Income)
NAL Investor Diversified	(Balanced)
Nalaco Diversified	(Balanced)
N Amer Growth RSP R	(Cdn. Equity)
N Amer Growth RSP B	(Fixed Income)
Equitable Life Ins. Co. Can.	(519) 886-5110
1 Westmount Road North	
Waterloo, Ontario	
N2J 4C7	
Equitable Life Canada	(Cdn. Equity)
Equit Life Cda Bd Mtge	(Fixed Income)

Fidelity Life Assurance Company (604) 734-1667
Box 34039
2165 W. Broadway
Vancouver, B.C.
V6J 1Z6

Fidelity Life Growth	(U.S. Equity)

Fiducie Du Quebec (Quebec Trust) (514) 286-5838
1 Complex Desjardins
C.P. 34
Montreal, Quebec
H5B 1E4

Fonds Desjard Actions	(Cdn. Equity)
Fonds Desjard Hypo	(Fixed Income)
Fonds Desjard Intl	(Int'l Equity)
Fonds Desjard Oblig	(Fixed Income)

Fiducie Pret Et Revenu (418) 692-1221
850 Place D'Youville
P.O. Box 2207
Quebec City, Quebec
G1K 7P3

Pret et Revenu Americain	(U.S. Equity)
Pret et Revenu Canadien	(Cdn. Equity)
Pret et Revenu Retraite	(Balanced)
Fonds d'Obligation	(Fixed Income)

First Canadian Mortgage Fund (416) 927-6285
17th Flr.
55 Bloor St. W.
Toronto, Ontario
M4W 3N5

First Canadian Mortgage	(Fixed Income)

First City Realfund (604) 685-2489
777 Hornby St.
Vancouver, B.C.
V6Z 1S4

First City Growth	(Cdn. Equity)
First City Income	(Fixed Income)
First City	(Special)

Fiscal Consultants Ltd. (416) 947-3712
19th Fl.
Royal Bank Plaza
Box 201
Toronto, Ontario
M5J 2J6

Fiscon	(Balanced)

Frazer, Leon, & Associates (416) 864-1120
Suite 2001
8 King St. E.
Toronto, Ontario
M5C 1B6

Associate Investors	(Cdn. Equity)

FutureFund Shares Inc. (416) 648-7363
Box 7290
Ancaster, Ontario
L9G 3N6

FutureFund Food	(Cdn. Equity)
FutureFund Golden	(Cdn. Equity)
FutureFund Life	(Cdn. Equity)
FutureFund Silver	(Cdn. Equity)
FutureFund Techno	(Cdn. Equity)
FutureFund Value	(Cdn. Equity)

General Trust Of Canada (514) 871-7100
1100 University Ave.
Montreal, Quebec
H3B 2G7

General Trust Mortgage	(Fixed Income)
Genl Tr Balanced	(Balanced)
Genl Tr Bond	(Fixed Income)
Genl Tr Cdn Equity	(Cdn. Equity)
Genl Tr Money Market	(Fixed Income)
Genl Tr U.S. Equity	(U.S. Equity)

Great Pacific Management (604) 669-1143
Ste. 1010
1200 Burrard St.
Vancouver, B.C.
V6Z 2C7

Synchrovest	(Balanced)

Great-West Life Assurance Company, The (204) 946-8536
60 Osborne St. N.
Winnipeg, Manitoba
R3C 3A5

Canadian Equity 2	(Cdn. Equity)

Greydanus Boeckh & Associates Inc. (519) 673-3020
300 Dundas Street
London, Ontario
N6B 2Y2

Hallmark Bond	(Fixed Income)
Hallmark Canadian	(Cdn. Equity)

Guaranty Trust Company Of Canada (416) 863-5043
4th Floor
625 Church St.
Toronto, Ontario
M4Y 2E8

Guaranty Tr Inv Equ R	(Cdn. Equity)
Guaranty Tr Inv Inc R	(Fixed Income)
Guaranty Tr Mgd Equ R	(Cdn. Equity)
Guaranty Tr Mgd Inc R	(Fixed Income)
Guaranty Trust Mortgage	(Fixed Income)

Guardian (416) 364-8341
Ste. 500
48 Yonge St.
Toronto, Ontario
M5E 1H3

Guardian Canadian	(Cdn. Equity)
Guardian Enterprise	(Cdn. Equity)
Guardian Growth	(U.S. Equity)
Guardian N American	(U.S. Equity)
Guardian Pref. Dividend	(Pref. Stock)
Guardian S-T Money	(Fixed Income)
Guardian World Equity	(Int'l Equity)

Guardian Timing Services (416) 863-1100
74 Victoria St.
Toronto, Ontario
M5C 2A5

Canadian Protected	(Cdn. Equity)
Salamander Trust	(U.S. Equity)

Hodgson Roberton Laing Ltd. (416) 368-1428
Ste. 1680
390 Bay St.
Toronto, Ontario
M5J 1L4

Waltaine Balanced	(Balanced)
Waltaine Convertible Pref.	(Pref. Stock)
Waltaine Instant $$	(Fixed Income)
Waltaine Pref Income	(Pref. Stock)

Horgan Tattersall Invest. Counsel Inc. (416) 979-1818
Ste. 1904
P.O. Box 95
20 Queen St. W.
Toronto, Ontario
M5H 3V2

Saxon Balanced	(Balanced)
Saxon Small Cap	(Cdn. Equity)
Saxon Stock	(Cdn. Equity)
Saxon World Growth	(Int'l Equity)

Hughes, King & Co.	(416) 863-0687
Ste. 2320	
390 Bay St.	
Toronto, Ontario	
M5H 2Y2	
Capstone	(Balanced)
Hume Financial Management Inc.	(416) 979-1707
Ste. 600	
70 University Ave.	
Toronto, Ontario	
M5J 2M4	
Hume Cdn. Bond Fund	(Fixed Income)
Hume Cdn. Equity Fund	(Cdn. Equity)
Hume Growth & Income	(Balanced)
Hume RRSP Growth & Inc.	(Balanced)
Imperial Life Assurance Co. of Canada	(416) 926-2974
95 St. Clair Ave. W.	
Toronto, Ontario	
M4W 1N7	
Impco Growth	(Cdn. Equity)
Impco Ret Growth	(Cdn. Equity)
Imperial Securities Ltd.	(204) 949-1200
1600, 363 Broadway Ave.	
Winnipeg, Manitoba	
R3C 3N9	
Imperial Mortgage	(Fixed Income)
Imperial Realty Growth	(Special)
Jones Heward Investment Mgmt. Inc.	(514) 286-7311
Ste. 2100	
770 Sherbrooke St. W.	
Montreal, Quebec	
H3A 1G1	
Jones Heward	(Cdn. Equity)
Jones Heward American	(Cdn. Equity)
Keltic Savings Corporation Ltd.	(902) 429-9911
1770 Market Street	
Halifax, Nova Scotia	
B3J 3M3	
Maritime Equity	(Cdn. Equity)

L'Assurance Vie Desjardins 200 Ave. Des Commondeurs Levis, Quebec G6V 6R2	(418) 835-2320
L'Assur-Vie Desjard Bond	(Fixed Income)
L'Assur-Vie Desjard Mtge	(Fixed Income)
L'Assur-Vie Desjard Stock	(Cdn. Equity)
L'Excellence Life Insurance Co. Ste. 717 276 Rue St. Jacques Montreal, Quebec H2Y 1N3	(514) 288-4043
London Life Insurance Co. 255 Dufferin Avenue London, Ontario N6A 4K1	(519) 432-5281
London Life Bond	(Fixed Income)
London Life Equity	(Cdn. Equity)
London Life Mortgage	(Fixed Income)
MONY Life Insurance Co. Of Canada 797 Don Mills Road Don Mills, Ontario M3C 1V2	(416) 429-2200
MONY Balanced	(Balanced)
MONY Bond	(Fixed Income)
MONY Canadian Growth	(Cdn. Equity)
MONY Global	(Int'l Equity)
MONY T-Bill	(Fixed Income)
Mackenzie Financial Corporation 150 Bloor St. West, 5th Floor Toronto, Ontario M5S 2X9	(416) 922-5322
Industrial American	(U.S. Equity)
Industrial Dividend	(Cdn. Equity)
Industrial Equity	(Cdn. Equity)
Industrial Global	(Int'l Equity)
Industrial Growth	(Cdn. Equity)
Industrial Horizon	(Cdn. Equity)
Industrial Income	(Fixed Income)
Industrial Pension	(Cdn. Equity)
Mackenzie Equity	(Cdn. Equity)
Mackenzie Mortgage	(Fixed Income)

Manulife Investment Management Corp. (416) 928-4329
2nd Fl., 250 Bloor St. W.
Toronto, Ontario
M5W 1E5

Manufacturers Bond	(Fixed Income)
Manufacturers Cap Gains	(Cdn. Equity)
Manufacturers Diversified	(Balanced)
Manufacturers Equity	(Cdn. Equity)
Manufacturers Short Term	(Fixed Income)

Marlborough Management Corp. Ltd. (416) 494-3039
P.O. Box 414
2 First Canadian Place
Toronto, Ontario
M5X 1J1

Marlborough	(Cdn. Equity)

Merritt Easton Rae Management Ltd. (604) 688-9531
Ste. 1703
1166 Alberni St.
Vancouver, B.C.
V6E 3Z3

MER Equity	(Cdn. Equity)
MER Growth	(Int'l Equity)
MER Money Market	(Fixed Income)

Metropolitan Group Ltd., The (403) 421-3934
2700, 10303 Jasper Ave.
Edmonton, Alberta
T5J 3N6

Metropolitan Bond	(Fixed Income)
Metropolitan Cdn	(Cdn. Equity)
Metropolitan Collective Mut	(U.S. Equity)
Metropolitan Growth	(Cdn. Equity)
Metropolitan Speculators	(U.S. Equity)
Metropolitan Venture	(U.S. Equity)

Montreal Life Insurance Company (514) 842-9151
630 Sherbrooke St.
Montreal, Quebec
H3A 1E4

Montreal Life	(Cdn. Equity)

Montreal Trustco Inc.	(514) 397-7000
1 Place Ville Marie	
Montreal, Quebec	
H3B 4A8	
Montreal Trust Equity	(Cdn. Equity)
Montreal Trust Income	(Fixed Income)
Montreal Trust Mortgage	(Fixed Income)
Mtl Trust RSP Eq Sec	(Cdn. Equity)
Mtl Trust RSP G'teed	(Fixed Income)
Mtl Trust RSP Inc Sec	(Fixed Income)
Mtl Trust RSP Mtge Sec	(Fixed Income)
Montreal Trust Int'l	(Int'l Equity)
Montreal Tr Dividend	(Pref. Stock)

Morgan Group, The	(416) 366-8999
Ste. 800	
55 Yonge St.	
Toronto, Ontario	
M5E 1J4	
Morgan Dividend	(Pref. Stock)
Morgan Growth	(Cdn. Equity)
Morgan Income	(Fixed Income)
Morgan Resource	(Cdn. Equity)
Morgan Worldwide	(Int'l Equity)

Multiple Opportunities Fund Mgmt. Ltd.	(604) 688-8151
Ste. 2020	
609 Granville St.	
Vancouver, B.C.	
V7Y 3A6	
Multiple Opportunities	(Cdn. Equity)

Mutual Life Assurance Company of Canada	(519) 888-2400
227 King Street South	
Waterloo, Ontario	
N2J 4C5	
Mutual Amerifund	(U.S. Equity)
Mutual Div. 25	(Balanced)
Mutual Div. 40	(Balanced)
Mutual Div. 55	(Balanced)
Mutual Dividend	(Pref. Stock)

Mutual Life Assurance Company of Canada (continued)	
Mutual Equity	(Cdn. Equity)
Mutual Life A	(Cdn. Equity)
Mutual Life B	(Cdn. Equity)
Mutual Life 2	(Fixed Income)
Mutual Money Market	(Fixed Income)

NW Fund Management Ltd. 12th Floor, 595 Howe St. Vancouver, B.C. V6C 2T5	(604) 689-1211
NW Canadian	(Cdn. Equity)
NW Equity	(U.S. Equity)
National Life Assurance Co. of Canada 522 University Ave. Toronto, Ontario M5G 1Y7	(416) 598-2122
Nat'l Life Equities	(Cdn. Equity)
Nat'l Life Fixed	(Fixed Income)
Nat'l Life of Cda	(Cdn. Equity)
National Trust Co. 21 King Street East Toronto, Ontario M5C 1B3	(416) 361-3611
Nat'l Tr. Feb. Pro	(Cdn. Equity)
Nat'l Tr. Jan. Pro	(Cdn. Equity)
Ntl. Trust Equity RSP	(Cdn. Equity)
Ntl. Trust Inc RSP	(Fixed Income)
Natrusco	(U.S. Equity)
Noram Capital Management Inc. Ste. 1400, 390 Bay Street Toronto, Ontario M5A 2H2	(614) 364-2642
Noram Cv Sec.	(Fixed Income)
PMF Management Ltd. 2700, 1 1st Canadian Place Box 379 Toronto, Ontario M5X 1J1	(416) 864-3500
Harvard Growth	(Cdn. Equity)
Pension Mutual	(Cdn. Equity)
Xanadu	(Cdn. Equity)
Pemberton Securities Ltd. 2400 Park Place 666 Burrard St. Vancouver, B.C. V6C 2C7	(604) 661-5920
Pacific Growth	(Cdn. Equity)
Pacific Retire Bal	(Balanced)
Pacific US Growth	(U.S. Equity)

Phillips, Hager & North Ltd. Ste. 1700 1055 W. Hastings St. Vancouver, B.C. V6E 2H3	(604) 684-4361
Phillips H & N Vintage	(Cdn. Equity)
Phillips H & N Bond	(Fixed Income)
Phillips H & N Cdn	(Cdn. Equity)
Phillips H & N Div	(Pref. Stock)
Phillips H & N Fund	(U.S. Equity)
Phillips H & N Retirement	(Cdn. Equity)
Procter Capital Mgmt. Inc. Ste. 1400, 110 Yonge St. Toronto, Ontario M5C 2S3	(416) 369-8984
Optimal Canadian	(Cdn. Equity)
Prudential Fund Mgmt. Canada 200 Consilium Place Scarborough, Ontario M1H 3E6	(416) 296-0777
Prudential Dividend	(Pref. Stock)
Prudential Growth	(Cdn. Equity)
Prudential Income	(Fixed Income)
Prudential Money Market	(Fixed Income)
Putnam Financial Services Inc. One Post Office Square Boston, MA 02109	(617) 292-1531
Putnam Health Science	(U.S. Equity)
Rabin, Budden Partners 194, 390 Bay St. Toronto, Ontario M5H 2Y2	(416) 865-1722
Rabin Budden Capital	(Balanced)
Rabin Budden Income	(Balanced)
Realcap Fund Mgmt. Ltd. Ste. 604, 2161 Yonge St. Toronto, Ontario M4S 3A5	(416) 486-7729
RealGrowth Active Inc.	(Fixed Income)
RealGrowth Amer. Trend	(U.S. Equity)
RealGrowth Cdn. Equity	(Cdn. Equity)

Royal Trustco Limited (416) 864-7000
P.O. Box 7500
Station A
Toronto, Ontario
M5W 1P9

Royal Tr Cdn Money Mkt	(Fixed Income)
Royal Tr Global Invest	(Int'l Equity)
Royal Trust Adv. Bal.	(Balanced)
Royal Trust Adv. Grth	(Balanced)
Royal Trust Adv. Inc.	(Balanced)
Royal Trust American	(U.S. Equity)
Royal Trust Bond	(Fixed Income)
Royal Trust Canadian	(Cdn. Equity)
Royal Trust Energy	(Cdn. Equity)
Royal Trust Japanese	(Special)
Royal Trust Mortgage	(Fixed Income)
Royal Trust Preferred	(Pref. Stock)

Royfund Ltd. (416) 865-0505
Ste. 2990
S. Tower
Royal Bank Plaza
Toronto, Ontario
M5J 2J2

Royfund Bond	(Fixed Income)
Royfund Equity	(Cdn. Equity)
Royfund Money Market	(Fixed Income)

Sagit Management Ltd. (604) 685-3193
Ste. 1650, 400 Burrard St.
Vancouver, B.C.
V6C 3A6

Cambridge Balanced	(Balanced)
Cambridge Growth	(Cdn. Equity)
Cambridge Resource	(Cdn. Equity)
Trans-Canada Equity	(Cdn. Equity)
Trans-Cda Shares B	(Cdn. Equity)
Trans-Cda Shares C	(Cdn. Equity)

Sceptre Investment Counsel (416) 360-4826
1200, 26 Wellington St. E.
Toronto, Ontario
M5E 1W4

Sceptre Balanced	(Balanced)
Sceptre Bond	(Fixed Income)
Sceptre Equity Fund	(Cdn. Equity)
Sceptre International	(Int'l Equity)

Seaboard Life Insurance Co. (604) 734-1667
2165 West Broadway
Vancouver, B.C.
V6K 4N5

Seaboard Life Accum 1	(U.S. Equity)
Seaboard Life Accum 2	(Fixed Income)

Sentinel Investment Management (416) 585-9111
Ste. 2309
150 King St. West
Toronto, Ontario
M5H 1J9

Sentinel Amer. Equity	(U.S. Equity)
Sentinel Canada Bond	(Fixed Income)
Sentinel Canada Equity	(Cdn. Equity)
Sentinel Global	(Int'l Equity)
Sentinel Money Market	(Fixed Income)

Sun Life Assurance Company of Canada (416) 595-7976
11th Floor
200 University Ave.
Toronto, Ontario
M5H 3C7

Sunfund	(Cdn. Equity)

Talvest Fund Management (514) 875-7040
Ste. 1900
Place Du Canada
Montreal, Quebec
H3B 2N2

Talvest American	(U.S. Equity)
Talvest Bond	(Fixed Income)
Talvest Diversified	(Balanced)
Talvest Growth	(Cdn. Equity)
Talvest Income	(Fixed Income)
Talvest Money	(Fixed Income)

Templeton Management Ltd., The (416) 364-4672
Box 4070, Stn. A
4 King St. W.
Toronto, Ontario
M5W 1M3

Templeton Canadian	(Cdn. Equity)
Templeton Growth	(Int'l Equity)

Toronto-Dominion Bank, The (416) 982-2373
Box 204, T-D Centre
Toronto, Ontario
M5K 1J3

TD's Green Line Mtge	(Fixed Income)

Tradex Investment Fund Ltd. (613) 233-3394
Room 401, 77 Metcalfe St.
Ottawa, Ontario
K1P 5L5

Tradex	(Cdn. Equity)

Trimark Investment Management Inc. (416) 862-2020
Ste. 935
1 First Canadian Place
Toronto, Ontario
M5X 1A6

Trimark	(Int'l Equity)
Trimark Canadian	(Cdn. Equity)
Trimark Interest	(Fixed Income)

20/20 Group Financial Inc. (416) 862-2020
2802, 79 Wellington St. W.
Toronto, Ontario
M5K 1H1

Cdn. Convertible Deb.	(Fixed Income)
Cdn. Convertible Pfd	(Pref. Stock)
Sunset Fund	(Balanced)

280 Broadway Holding Corp. (204) 949-8240
280 Broadway Ave.
Winnipeg, Manitoba
R3C 3B6

Investors Bond	(Fixed Income)
Investors Cdn Equity	(Cdn. Equity)
Investors Dividend	(Pref. Stock)
Investors Global Fund	(Int'l Equity)
Investors Growth	(Cdn. Equity)
Investors Int'l	(U.S. Equity)
Investors Japanese	(Special)
Investors Money Mkt	(Fixed Income)
Investors Mortgage	(Fixed Income)
Investors Mutual	(Balanced)
Investors Real Property	(Special)
Investors Retirement	(Cdn. Equity)

United Financial Management Ltd. (416) 598-5181
Ste. 1202
200 King St. W.
Toronto, Ontario
M5H 3W8

United Accumulative	(Int'l Equity)
United Accum Retire	(Cdn. Equity)
United American	(U.S. Equity)
United Mtge	(Fixed Income)
United Security	(Fixed Income)
United Venture	(U.S. Equity)
United Venture Retire	(Cdn. Equity)

Universal Group of Funds, The Ste. 1218 401 Bay St. Toronto, Ontario M5H 2Y4	(416) 364-1145
Univ Svgs American	(U.S. Equity)
Universal Savings Eq	(Cdn. Equity)
Universal Savings Global	(Int'l Equity)
Universal Savings Inc	(Fixed Income)
Univ Svgs Natl Res	(Cdn. Equity)
Universal Savings Pacific	(Special)
Van City Investment Services Ltd. 515 West Tenth Avenue Vancouver, B.C. V5Z 4A8	(604) 877-7000
Ethical Growth	(Cdn. Equity)
Walwyn Stodgell Cochran Murray Ltd. Ste. 800 70 University Ave. Toronto, Ontario M5J 2M5	(416) 591-6000
Capital Growth	(Cdn. Equity)
Walwyn Bond	(Fixed Income)
Walwyn Cdn Equity	(Cdn. Equity)
Walwyn Int'l	(Int'l Equity)
Walwyn Money Market	(Fixed Income)
Walwyn Option Equity	(Int'l Equity)
Walwyn Preferred	(Pref. Stock)
Walwyn Venture	(Cdn. Equity)
Western Investment Services Co. Ltd. 10155—120th St., 2nd fl. Edmonton, Alberta T5K 2A2	(403) 488-0677
Western Growth	(Cdn. Equity)
Wong, M.K., & Associates Ltd. Ste. 2520 1066 Hastings St. Vancouver, B.C. V6E 3X1	(604) 699-455
Lotus	(Balanced)
One Decision	(Balanced)

Worldwide Capital Management Ltd. 1500, 2 Bloor St. West Toronto, Ontario M5W 1A1	(416) 927-0233
Global Strategy Americas	(Int'l Equity)
Global Strategy Corp.	(Int'l Equity)
Global Strategy Europe	(Int'l Equity)
Global Strategy Far East	(Int'l Equity)
Global Strategy Fund	(Int'l Equity)

Index